The Bible
and
Modern Criticism

Sir Robert Anderson, K.C.B., LL.D.

With a Preface

By The Right Reverend
Handley C. G. Moule, D.D.
Bishop of Durham

Fifth Edition
1905

London: Hodder and Stoughton
27 Paternoster Row

Copyright 2016 Trumpet Press
Trumpet Press, Lawton, OK

Copyright © 2016 by Trumpet Press All rights reserved

ISBN-13: 978-1535316095
ISBN-10: 1535316098

Trumpet Press is a member of the Christian Small Publishers Association (CSPA).

Table of Contents

Preface 8
Chapter 1 12
    The purpose of this book. Appeals to authority barred. The Martyrs. Shallow and jaunty skepticism. Prof. Cheyne's *Encyclopedia Biblica*. Credulity of the critics.

Chapter 2 18
    The Bible a human book. Rationalists and Revolutionists. Dean Alford quoted. The *Encyclopedia Biblica* and *Hastings' Bible Dictionary*. Are the Gospels inspired? Police officers v. the Saints. Quotations from Goldwin Smith; and from Matthew Arnold. The question again restated.

Chapter 3 25
    Origin of the Higher Criticism. The Reformation and the Bible. Neglect of Scripture. How to meet the critics. Professors and book scholars. The "Ptolemaic System." The letter of a penitent skeptic.

Chapter 4 34
    Charles II. Faith and morals. Robertson Smith's apostasy. History and aims of the Higher Criticism. Prof. Cheyne. The Higher Criticism not a preserve of Hebraists. The Pentateuch. Isaiah II. Harnack on the New Testament. The nature of prophecy.

Chapter 5 43
    Charles Reade on miracles. Christianized skeptic s. Prayer, and a silent heaven. The Divinity of Christ the real question. Matthew Arnold on miracles. The rejection of Christ and of the Bible.

Chapter 6 50
    Presumption for a written Revelation. "Brainless idiots," and great lawyers. Christianity rests on a Divine revelation. The Old Testament accredited by Christ. Christ discredited by the critics. Why not have two wives? Kenosis theories. The two sides of the tapestry.

Chapter 7 58
The method of the inspiration. David and his sin: Carlyle's testimony. Verbal inspiration, facts and fallacies. Yahweh or Jehovah. The human element in miracles. Verbal inspiration discussed.

Chapter 8 67
Verbal inspiration, continued. Dependent on translations. "Words are but counters: "Eternal." "Priest." Original records lost. Various readings. The Revised Version of New Testament. The "Herald Angels' Song."

Chapter 9 76
The Creation story of Genesis. The Gladstone-Huxley controversy. The Times correspondence of 1892. The teaching of Genesis and the creation "day."

Chapter 10 87
The Book of Daniel. Questions of language. "Historical Errors." The Canon. The "Seventy Weeks."

Chapter 11 94
The Book of Jonah. An Irish story. Whale or shark. The miracle. Accredited by Christ. Historical difficulties.

Chapter 12 101
Moral difficulties: Queen Victoria and a homicide. Destruction of the Canaanites. The Jews and the world. The price of Araunah's threshing-floor. The chronology of the Bible.

Chapter 13 109
The Higher Criticism and the New Testament: a conversation with a Higher Critic. Bishop Gore's school. Inspiration of the Gospels. The Lord accredited the Old Testament. He assured the inspiration of the New Testament. The Epistles. The Apocalypse.

Chapter 14 118
Vaccination: the skepticism virus. The "Ptolemaic System" of Bible Study. The First and Fourth Gospels as read on this system.

Chapter 15 123
The true exegesis of the Gospels. The scope of Matthew. The Lord's testimony. The crisis of the Ministry. The parables of chapter 13. Other effects of His rejection.

Chapter 16 135
The Parousia. Amateur detectives, and ignorance of the Higher Critics. A conference on the Gospel, and the doctrine of the types.

Chapter 17 140
Errors in the Gospels: an Irish story. The blind men outside Jericho. Theudas's insurrection. "This generation shall not pass." The Inscription on the Cross.

Chapter 18 146
The Last Supper and the day of the Crucifixion. The "Preparation." The day of the "First-fruits." The Calendar a prophecy: Doctrine of the Festivals.

Chapter 19 156
Summary and conclusion. The critics and their competence. Practical advice. "Post-mortem talk." The Genesis "documents." The origin of Higher Criticism. Kenosis teaching of the Higher Criticism, and the issue at stake.

Appendix 166
Note I: Isolated Texts relied on by the Higher Critics
Note II: The Revised Version of the New Testament
Note III: "Three Days and Three Nights"
Note IV: The Genealogies of our Lord
Note V: The Kingdom of Heaven, the Kingdom of God, and the Church

Other works by Sir. Robert Anderson:

The Buddha of Christendom. A Book for the Present Crisis

The Silence of God. Sixth Edition

Human Destiny. Fifth Edition

The Coming Prince; or, The Seventy Weeks of Daniel.

Daniel in the Critics' Den. A Reply to Prof. Driver and the (late) Dean of Canterbury.

The Gospel and its Ministry. A Handbook of Evangelical Truth. Twelfth Edition, Revised

Pseudo-Criticism; or, The Higher Criticism and its Counterfeit

"For Us Men": Chapters on Redemption Truths

A Doubter's Doubts about Science and Religion

NOTE from the publisher:

Sir Robert Anderson put his Scotland Yard detective skills to use at understanding the Bible for many years, and authored many noted books on the Bible. In this book he analyzes those "experts" who analyze the text of the Bible.

This book provides evidence against the Higher Criticism of the Bible by such people as Westcott and Hort and other nonbelievers. Yes, nonbelievers are being trusted to give us the correct text of the Bible, but they should not be trusted, as they are sabotaging the Bible text.

This book was highly praised when first published and went through five editions, but it is ignored by the so-called scholars of today.

This book was formatted to look just like the eBook edition. Since eBooks do not have pages, all footnotes are placed below each paragraph.

Preface

The following chapters have little need of any prefatory remarks of mine. Alike their subject, their material, and the author's handling of that material, will command the attention of a wide circle of readers, and will indeed repay it. But I am honored by the request to prefix these few paragraphs, and I obey.

I have the author's full leave to say that there are details in the matter of the book, and even certain aspects of the treatment, from which I hold myself detached. For example, I cannot commit myself to concurrence with the whole of the important but incidental criticism of the Revised Version. I am in suspense on some main items of Sir R. Anderson's discussion of outlines of the prophetic future, while I regard with profound respect the ability and the suggestiveness of the discussion. Again, I must dissociate myself from certain passages which reflect upon the animus of some representatives of the New Criticism with a severity I cannot follow. Among both leaders and followers in that school I reckon some much-respected friends, of whose reverent and Christian aims I am sure; and that fact is continually with me in any expression of the profound anxiety with which I view the tendency of the school.

But when I have said this, I am amply free, as I am earnestly willing, to avow my mental and spiritual sympathy with the great envoi of this remarkable book.

What is the book? It is the free and (to use the word in its best sense) popular presentation of the results of an independent study of the New Criticism, as actually put before us in representative works, done by a student entirely free from professional bias, and trained in a severe school of legal and judicial investigation to sift witnesses and weigh evidence. It is an example of exactly the sort of work which, in my opinion, the Church needs in an eminent degree, and which is, I fear, lamentably rare today - the careful study of religious problems by laymen at once open-minded and devout. In the best specimens of such study there is often, to my thinking, a quite peculiar value; a fresh and bracing air of thought all their own, a faculty for throwing wholesome light upon subjects tangled by the over-handling of experts.

Experts, as Sir R. Anderson often pertinently reminds us, are by no means, as such, good judges.

"At the bar we sometimes find a man's logic swamped by his learning; and so it is in theology." Thus wrote the late Lord Hatherley to me, in a private letter, thirty years ago, and went on to say that he wished for leisure to illustrate the poor reasoning power of some of the greatest German literati. Lord Hatherley was one of our first masters of evidence. He was a life-long student of the Holy Scriptures. And the modest Introduction to his *Continuity* is a fine summing- up in favor of their properly supernatural character. That book was a noble lay contribution to the defense of faith. Another master of the practical application of legal science gives us another here.

And is there not a cause? The attitude towards Holy Scripture of a vast deal of cultured thought and responsible teaching at present offers assuredly a problem which it is idle to dismiss as if it were not portentous. By whatever process it has come to be, teachers and disciples far and wide now regard the Old Testament (to speak of it only for the instant) from an angle totally- different (I use the words deliberately) from that taken by our Lord Jesus Christ, alike before and after His Resurrection from the dead. To Him, tempted, teaching, suffering, dying, risen, "it is written" was a formula of infinite import. The principle this expressed lay at the heart of His teaching. It is not too much to say that it belonged to the pulse, to the vital breath, of His message to others, and, what is mysteriously yet more, to His certainty about Himself. But in wide circles of our Christendom it is now openly or tacitly taken to be out of date, to be narrow, to be uncultured, to make much of "it is written;" as if an appeal to a definite supernatural book- revelation were a thing discredited and to be given up.

If a severe necessity of irrefragable truth demands this, be it so. But let not the conclusion be reached, or rested in, light-heartedly, and smoothly decorated with the comfortable phraseology current in articles and reviews. The conclusion, if true, is portentous. It is a confession that on a matter central in His message our Master was much mistaken. He appears thus as not merely capable of nescience; that is a very different matter; the most cautious, the most worshipping, theology may hold that He consented, in His Humanity, to limitations of His conscious knowledge and to silence outside those bounds. But here He appears as ignorant with that sort of ignorance which profoundly impairs the whole value of a teacher-- the ignorance of the man who does not know where his knowledge ends, and so makes confident affirmations, and draws confident inferences, where his basis as to facts is unsound.

Such a fallible Christ lies open to the suspicion of fallibility on other matters than the nature and integrity of the Old Testament; and reasonably. The theology which denies the Lord abnormal knowledge of facts of the past is only consistent when it extends its denial to the future, and takes *cum grano* the New Testament doctrine of His Return, which is a matter either of revelation, or of the vaguest and most impalpable forecast. Such extensions have undoubtedly come to be freely made within Christian circles; and not only in the *Encyclopedia Biblica*.

If these conclusions be demanded by irrefutable fact, let them be made, and accepted. But not (I repeat) light-heartedly, and as if we were the freer for them, and could talk glibly about them in the best modern style. Let us make them with a groan, and take care to carve no more the unauthentic promise on the tombs of our beloved.

But first let us be absolutely sure that our detraction from the complete infallibility of the Lord Jesus Christ has infallible grounds. Let us take particular care to be sure that its basis is no *a priori* theory of the genesis of Religion, which may even already be on its way to discredit in the court of knowledge and thought.

Wisely does Sir R. Anderson disclaim any neat theory of inspiration; as wisely does he emphasize the true, the profound, humanity of the Bible. But all the more is he in the right when he analyzes with the utmost rigor the flaws in the modern analysis of the Book, and calls reverent attention to the mysterious facts of its organic structure, and gives us both precept and example for an always deepening study of its hidden treasures.

The matter is one where, while the fairness of controversy must be guarded, as ever, its mere courtesies may not always be in place. For the question is of tremendous urgency. "We are contending for our all."

Handley Dunelm

Prefatory Note

The title of this book is borrowed from *The Times*. It was the heading given to an important correspondence, in which I was permitted to take a prominent part, some years ago, in the columns of the leading journal.

I will only add that my obligations to the Bishop of Durham are much greater even than they here appear to be. And I am deeply indebted to two other friends for valuable help.

I would specially name the Rev. Robert Sinker, D.D., of Trinity College, Cambridge.

R. A.

Note to The Fourth Edition

The following paragraphs from the "Note to the Second Edition" contain all that seems necessary by way of preface in issuing a Fourth Edition of this work. Or if I add anything, it will be merely to express my appreciation of the generosity and favor with which the book has been received by Christians generally.

Any hostile criticisms which have been offered on statements contained in these pages are fully answered by other portions of the book itself. And my apology for all "sins of omission" will be found in the opening sentence of Chapter 19. Moreover, a detailed reply to certain favorite theories of the critics, which I am said to have left unnoticed, would have no weight with the critics themselves, and is not needed by those for whom the book is intended.

Take ex. gr. the theory as to the late date of the Books of Moses. Even if the case made out by the critics were as strong as it is weak, it would be refuted by the single fact that the Pentateuch was emphatically the Bible of the Samaritans. That the Samaritans would have accorded such peculiar and unbounded reverence to purely Jewish Books, and to Jewish Books of a period long after the captivity of the ten tribes of the house of Israel, is a figment unworthy of serious discussion. Its acceptance by the Higher Critics gives proof that they are incapable of dealing with evidence.

R.A.

Chapter 1

In these days of unrest many Christians are distressed by doubts whether the Bible may be received with the settled and simple faith accorded to it in the past. They have been corrupted or disturbed by the Christianized skepticism which prevails; and, to use an apt illustration, their anchor has dragged and they are drifting. It may be, therefore, that one who has known similar experiences, and is no stranger to such doubts, may be able in some measure to help others who are thus troubled.

In the history of Christendom, Churches of every name, and —as judged from the inquirer's point of view—of every degree of orthodoxy or of error, have agreed in regarding the Bible as a divinely inspired and infallible revelation. No detailed proof of this statement is necessary here, for not only is its truth acknowledged, but the grounds on which the historic belief is challenged lie entirely apart from all appeals to authority.

And no appeals of this kind shall prejudice my discussion of the question. Being by temperament and habit a skeptic , they weigh but little with me personally, and I have found a firmer basis for my faith. But there are two sides to this. Many there are who loudly protest against appeals to authority, and yet their own faith in Holy Scripture has been jettisoned solely because contemporary scholars of a certain school have declared against the old beliefs.

If authority is to decide the question, the issue is not doubtful. For every one of these apostles of unfaith, scholars of equal eminence may be cited on the other side. And behind them is the overwhelming testimony of "the whole congregation of Christian people dispersed throughout the whole world," who, all down the ages until recent times, have spoken with one voice upon this subject. If our nineteenth century critics are to be listened to, are these to be refused a hearing?

Nor can we forget the martyrs, who in unnumbered thousands— their names are written in heaven, but earth has kept no record of them— braved every kind of agony of mind and body that could be devised by religious hate—the most fiendish type of hate that fallen human nature knows. It was not strong men only who swelled their ranks. Weak women there were, too, and even children were not wanting. What was the secret of their triumph? Was it "the general sense of Scripture corrected in the light of modern research"? In the solitude of the dungeon and amidst the horrors of the torture chamber they were sustained by words from the Bible, which they took to be the words of God. Words, for example, such as these: "He hath said 'I will never leave thee nor forsake thee,' so that we may boldly say 'The Lord is my helper,' and 'I will not fear what man shall do unto me.' "But further knowledge and higher culture, forsooth, would have taught them that the words, "I will never leave thee nor forsake thee," are but an inaccurate quotation from a book which is now known not to have the authority that for thousands of years has been attributed to it; and that the added words are by "a sub-apostolic writer" whose treatise is separated by no hard and fast lines from similar writings outside the canon of Scripture.

So at least the critics would have us believe. But if we are to shut out the testimony of the martyrs, as well as that of "Christian people dispersed throughout the whole world," including contemporary scholars equal in fame to the critics, let us not be guilty of the unfairness and stupidity of assuming at the start that the critics are right. Let us refuse appeals to authority on either side, and deal with the question on its merits.

And this leads me, by way of further preface, to enter a protest against the shallow and jaunty skepticism of the day. The issues at stake are tremendous, and in dealing with them no degree of earnestness and solemnity can be excessive. One of the apostles of unfaith will tell us that "Milton and Shakespeare and Bacon, and Canticles and the Apocalypse and the Sermon on the Mount, and the eighth chapter of Romans are all inspired." That "there is a true inspiration in the instinct of the owl; that it is heard in the rushing of the wind; that it is seen in the springing of a blade of grass; that it murmurs along the streams that flow among the hills." Such trifling is deplorable. A mere peasant can see that if this be the meaning of inspiration, we must fall back upon natural religion. If the Bible be nothing more than what such writers see it to be, Christianity rests on no rational basis. This is no argument in proof that the Bible is inspired; but it ought to check all levity in dealing with the question. If my bank notes are forgeries, I am a ruined bankrupt; this does not prove them genuine, but it will prevent my parting with them unless compelled to do so by cogent proof that they are counterfeit.

But it will be said, perhaps, that in England at least no scholar of repute among the Higher Critics assumes a position which is really destructive of Christianity. Though they challenge the authority of various books of the Canon, they leave untouched all that is vital. Let us test this. The *Encyclopedia Biblica* is the most recent exposition of the views of this school. Its editor is Professor Cheyne, of Oxford, [1] a man who is a teacher of teachers, and whose name stands high as an authority on all subjects of this kind. The following extracts are culled from the article on the Gospels:—

> 1] To give him his full title, the Rev. T. K. Cheyne, M.A., D.D., Oriel Professor of the Interpretation of Holy Scripture at Oxford, and formerly Fellow of Balliol College; Canon of Rochester.

"Several of the reported sayings of Jesus clearly bear the impress of a time which he did not live to see" (section 136).

"The conclusion is inevitable that even the one Evangelist whose story in any particular case involves less of the supernatural than that of the others, is still very far from being entitled on that account to claim implicit acceptance of his narrative" (section 137).

"With reference to the resurrection of Jesus . . . the appearance in Jerusalem to the two women is almost universally given up. . . . The statements as to the empty sepulchre are to be rejected" (section 138).

"As for the feeding of the five thousand and the four thousand, so also for the withering of the fig tree, we still possess a clue to the way in which the narrative arose out of a parable" (section 142).

"It is very conceivable that a preacher on the death of Jesus may have said, purely figuratively, that then was the veil of the temple rent in twain."

"We must endeavour to ascertain how many, and still more what sorts of cures were effected by Jesus. It is quite possible for us to regard as historical only those of the class which even at the present day physicians are able to effect by psychical methods,—as more especially cures of mental maladies.

"It is not at all difficult to understand how the contemporaries of Jesus, after seeing some wonderful deed or deeds wrought by him which they regarded as miracles, should have credited him with every other kind of miraculous power without distinguishing, as the modern mind does, between those maladies which are amenable to psychical influences and those which are not. It is also necessary to bear in mind that the cure may often have been only temporary" (section 144).

No one who reads the foregoing extracts will be surprised at the writer's raising the question "whether any credible elements were to be found in the Gospels at all." "All the more emphatically" therefore he enumerates nine passages which he saves from the general wreck. [1] These, he goes on to say, "might be called the foundation pillars of a truly scientific life of Jesus; . . . they prove that in the person of Jesus we have to do with a completely human being, and that the Divine is to be sought in Him only in the form in which it is capable of being found in a man; they also prove that He really did exist, and that the Gospels contain at least some absolutely trustworthy facts concerning him."[2]

> 1] These are, Matt. 11:5 (Luke 7:22); Matt 12:31, f.; Mark 3:21; 6:5, f.; 8:12; 8:14-21; 10:17, f.; 13:22, and 15:34 (Matt 27:46).
>
> 2] section 138. I trust no one will judge me harshly for thus reproducing here this blasphemy. I deem it a duty to do so because so many Christians are trifling with the infidel movement in ignorance of its aims and methods. The article cited is not by the Editor.

Any person of ordinary intelligence can see that this teaching makes an end of Christianity altogether. The public facts of the life of the great Rabbi of Nazareth are not questioned. What the world saw nineteen centuries ago, the world believes today. And those facts, combined with His traditional teaching, may be made the basis of a Christianized Buddhism which would possibly be the best of all human religions. But Christianity is not a human religion, but a divine revelation of transcendental truths and of facts that are of such a nature that no amount of mere human testimony could accredit them.

> "The first of these facts, upon which all the rest depend, is that the Nazarene was the Son of God. The founder of Rome was believed to be the divinely begotten child of a vestal Virgin. And in the old Babylonian mysteries a similar parentage was ascribed to the martyred son of the Queen of Heaven. What reason have we then for distinguishing the birth at Bethlehem from these and other kindred legends of the ancient world?"' (*The Buddha of Christendom*, p. 96.)

He was, we read, "declared to be the Son of God ... by the resurrection from the dead." But even this is filched from us: "the statements as to the empty sepulcher are to be rejected." Some of the German skeptics formerly accepted the public proofs of the resurrection, and therefore their teaching seemed to imply belief in that supreme miracle. Among the initiated, however, they explained the "resurrection " by denying the death. The cumulative evidence that the Nazarene was seen alive after the Crucifixion was proof that He had not really died. As He hung upon the cross He swooned, and before He recovered consciousness He was laid in the sepulcher. The superstitious imagination of the disciples, unnerved by the terrible ordeal they had suffered, gave a color to the facts; and ere the Gospel narratives came to be written, the resurrection legend had gained shape and substance. But the Oxford infidelity of today is far in advance of German infidelity of half a century ago. The Gospels are now romance pure and simple, with no foundation save the public facts, and a few isolated passages which prove that the great Teacher was really an historic personage.

And the objective foundations of our faith being thus destroyed, Christianity in its subjective phase is the merest superstition. Not one of the nine authentic passages, thus saved from the wreck, will avail us here. Faith is impossible. We must fall back on mere opinions. And he who would die for his opinions is a silly fanatic. The man who has nothing to rest upon but Professor Cheyne's Bible, and yet believes in "the forgiveness of sins, the resurrection of the body, and the life everlasting" is obviously a credulous person who would believe anything.

Chapter 2

No error lives unless it rests upon some element of truth. And the Higher Criticism owes its vitality to the fact that the Bible is a human book. The written Word is the counterpart of the Living Word. And the ancient controversies about the Christ have in modern times their counterpart in controversies about the Scriptures. Human nature being what it is, men in their eagerness to escape from one error are prone to rush into another. The old Gnostic heresy, in that development of it which maintained that everything material was evil, tended to the denial of the humanity of Christ. This led to an assertion of His humanity in a way which encroached upon the doctrine of His Divine nature. In the swinging of the pendulum of opinion the mean of truth was lost, and the two extremes were manifested in the practical denial that He was man and the practical denial that He was God.

So has it been with the Bible. The rationalism of the post-Reformation age asserted or assumed that the Bible was only and altogether a human book. An unintelligent orthodoxy maintained that it was only and altogether Divine. And both these extremes find advocates in England today. The sympathies of the Christian are naturally with those who give an exclusive prominence to the Divine side of Scripture. But our sympathies must not betray us into a participation in their error. Christ was not half man and half God; He was absolutely human, and yet absolutely Divine. And so is it also with the Bible. While it is absolutely the Word of God, it is also the most thoroughly human book in the world. Hence its amazing power over the hearts and minds of men. And our condemnation of the Higher Critics must not blind us to the fact that if they have not actually rescued this truth, they have brought it into prominence and made it real. But on the other hand our debt to them in this regard cannot be allowed to outweigh, or even to palliate, the evil of their system.

Chapter 2

We owe a debt to the red revolutionists of a century ago. But what lives in our memory is not the good which has resulted from their work, but the excesses they committed in achieving it. The German rationalists and their imitators and disciples of the *Encyclopedia Biblica* are in their own sphere on a par with the men of the Reign of Terror in France. To teach us that a queen is but a woman, we do not need the shameful spectacle of the bloodstained guillotine, the debasing lesson that, as Edmund Burke expressed it, "a woman is but an animal, and not the highest kind of animal either." And we can know, and rejoice in the knowledge, that the Bible is thoroughly, exquisitely human, without having to suffer the ordeal of seeing our adorable Lord thus patronized and blasphemed, and the holy writings which testify to Him perverted and degraded.

If a surgeon thinks only of his patient's dignity and rank, a trembling hand perchance may unfit him for his task. But the man who plunges his knife into a living human body as though it were the carcass of a brute, is no better than a butcher. And so we can criticize the Bible on its human side without ever allowing ourselves to forget that it is "the living and eternally abiding Word of God"; but we search in vain the writings of the critics for any indication of the reverence which is its due.

How different the spirit which animates them from that which characterized that great expositor and divine, Dean Alford! Here are the closing words of his New Testament Commentary:—

> "I have now only to commend to my gracious God and Father this feeble attempt to explain the most mysterious and glorious portion of His revealed Scriptures: and with it, this my labor of now eighteen years, herewith completed. I do so with humble thankfulness, but with a sense of utter weakness before the power of His Word, and inability to sound the depths even of its simplest sentence. May He spare the hand which has been put forward to touch His Ark."

If the critics know anything of the spirit of these words they are consummate masters of the art of concealing their emotions.

It will be said, perhaps, that the book I have cited does not fairly represent the teaching of the Critical School. If the objection refers to those who belong to the Church of England, it is well founded. It is happily unusual for English gentlemen to give solemn pledges in entering upon positions of influence and trust, and then to flout and violate those pledges.' [1] But the *Encyclopedia Biblica* is in this sphere what the *enfant terrible* is in the family circle— it gives out unblushingly what many of the critics themselves would deprecate.

> 1] Ordination in the Church of England is conditioned on an unequivocal reply to the question, "Do you unfeignedly believe all the Canonical Scriptures of the Old and New Testament?"

The difference between the work in question and the more conservative and cautious *Dictionary of the Bible* edited by Dr. Hastings, to which Professor Driver, of Oxford, has lent his name, is that the one represents the Bible as error and romance mingled with truth, and the other as truth mingled with romance and error. For certain purposes the distinction is a real one, but here it is immaterial. For the question I have raised is whether the old-fashioned belief in the inspiration of Scripture can be maintained; and the main purpose of every work emanating from these writers is, as they would say, to remove the difficulties and dangers which the historic view of inspiration is supposed to create.

The one set of writers hand me a purse of coins, with an assurance that most of them are genuine. The other set of writers hand me a purse of coins, with a warning that most of them are counterfeit. But as I am unable to distinguish between the base coins and the gold, honesty forbids my trading with any of them, and therefore all my seeming wealth is practically useless. In either case the Bible is like a lottery bag, from which blanks and prizes must be drawn at random. If the one section of the critics may be trusted, the prizes abound; if the other section be right, the blanks predominate. But in either case, I repeat, faith is impossible, and therefore Christianity is destroyed.

I am not prejudging the question raised in my opening sentences: I am merely seeking to state it clearly and intelligently, and to enter a protest against levity in dealing with it. Let me put it in a concrete form: Are the Gospels, as the critics of every section tell us, merely human documents, based in part upon the memory of the writers, in part upon earlier records, in part upon oral traditions of the great Teacher's acts and words? Or are they, as Christians have heretofore believed, God-breathed Scriptures — the Word of God, by which the sinner may be born again, and the disciple may "grow in grace" and be "thoroughly furnished unto all good works"?

For example, may I trust the record contained in the third chapter of John? Not one of the disciples, we may be sure, was with the Lord when Nicodemus "came to Him by night." But, waiving that, what reason have we for supposing the interview is reported accurately? Very many people bear testimony that the words of the 14th, 15th, and 16th verses have been the means of producing in them that change of heart and life which the Bible calls being born again and being converted. But this implies that the words are not a mere fallible human record of a conversation alleged to have occurred between Christ and a Pharisee; but an infallibly inspired proclamation of Divine love to the lost, bringing everlasting life to all who believe in the Son of God. Now these two views stand entirely apart. One or other of them must be false. And which is it?

Take another case. Who vouches for the record of the scene enacted, and the words spoken by our Divine Lord, in Gethsemane? The three disciples who alone were present lay sleeping, wholly unconscious of the solemnity and significance of that awful hour. And the critics tell us that when at last they awoke they were so utterly dazed and stupid that they mistook the shimmer of the moonlight for an angelic apparition. Either the record is in the strictest sense inspired, or else it is no better than a fairy tale.

I have often wondered at the definiteness with which some police officers could repeat the identical language used by a prisoner on arrest, or in the course of a railway journey. In these men habit and training have developed a natural aptitude for accuracy. Eliminate, as the critics do, the work of the Spirit of God, and I have no hesitation in saying that if I had on one side the testimony of the police inspectors of the department I recently controlled, and on the other side that of all the apostles and evangelists, I should trust to the memory of the officers rather than to that of the saints. But an officer's duty requires that as soon as practicable after hearing any important statement he shall record it in writing; and if some months after the event I found that he had neglected that duty, and yet that he professed to repeat the exact words used in a prolonged conversation, I should lose all confidence both in his judgment and in his truthfulness.

And now to explain my parable. What importance am I to attach to the record of prolonged discourses supposed to have been spoken by the Lord; such, for example, as "the Sermon on the Mount," [1] "the Second Sermon on the Mount," [2] or the Lord's last words before the Passion, [3] recorded more than forty years after they were uttered? If the Gospels are not inspired in the strictest sense in which theologians speak of inspiration, these records are worthless. Indeed if the critics are right, the Evangelists belonged to the class of "chatty" and imaginative people whose presence is often welcome in social life, but always dreaded in the witness chair of a Court of Justice. It avails nothing to plead that the apostles were very holy men. Experience teaches us that very holy men, and very learned men, too, may be very silly. And if some of the critics are to be believed, silliness was as marked a characteristic of the Evangelists as holiness. [4]

> 1] Matt, 5., 6., and 7.
>
> 2] Ibid. 24. and 25.
>
> 3] John 14., 15., 16., and 17.
>
> 4] Indeed the patronizing tone of their criticisms implies that if men of their own type had been employed to write the Gospels, the record would have been free from the defects and errors which now mar it.

In all this, I repeat, I am not "laying down the law," but only "stating the case." Neither am I specially addressing those who sympathize with my conclusions. I appeal to all intelligent and fair-minded thinkers. The only kind of person I wish to ignore is the fool. We all know the sort of morbidly active-brained child who will pull a valuable watch to pieces, and then tell us with a smile that "there was nothing in it but wheels and things." He has his counterpart in the foreign infidel type of scholar, who, albeit as ignorant of man and his needs as a monk, and as ignorant of God and His ways as a monkey, sets himself with a light heart to tear the Bible to pieces. If the Bible must be given up, it is a disaster unparalleled in the history of Christendom.

> "The Reformation was a tremendous earthquake; it shook down the fabric of mediaeval religion, and as a consequence of the disturbance in the religious sphere, filled the world with revolutions and wars. But it left the authority of the Bible unshaken, and men might feel that the destructive process had its

Chapter 2

limit, and that adamant was still beneath their feet . But a world which is intellectual and keenly alive to the significance of these questions, reading all that is written about them with almost passionate avidity, finds itself brought to a crisis the character of which any one may realize by distinctly presenting to himself the idea of existence without a God."

These are the words of one [1] whose thorough sympathy with "science and criticism " could not blind him to the gravity of the crisis they have caused. Fresh and vigorous minds will press on where these teachers now timidly shrink back. And while a religious agnosticism may afford a doubtful refuge to the cultured classes, agnosticism with no element whatever of religion will engulf the unthinking multitude. Men may well start back at sight of such a goal.

1] Professor Goldwin Smith.

Hear another witness, a veritable apostle of unfaith. In answer to the infidel taunt that Christianity was "an awful plague," because its success involved the ruin of Roman civilization, Matthew Arnold writes: "It was worthwhile to have that civilization ruined fifty times over, for the sake of planting Christianity through Europe in the only form in which it could then be planted there." [1] And surely some feeling of deep regret, if not of misgiving about his own position and influence, must have touched his heart as he penned the lines:—

1] *God and the Bible* (Preface).

"The sea of Faith
Was once, too, at the full, and round earth's shore
Lay like the folds of a bright girdle furl'd;
But now I only hear
Its melancholy, long, withdrawing roar."

I have already restated my thesis: let me do so once again. We shall gain nothing by dealing with generalities. Let us open the Gospels at the last of the test passages I have cited, and take the well-known words:—

"Let not your heart be troubled: ye believe in God, believe also in me.

"In my Father's house are many mansions: if it were not so, I would have told you. I go to prepare a place for you.

"And if I go and prepare a place for you, I will come again and receive you unto myself; that where I am, there ye may be also."

May we still use such words as these to comfort us in sorrow, and to cheer and strengthen us when life is failing, and its supreme crisis is drawing near? May we still trust them, as our fathers did, as a message from the heart and lips of our Savior and Lord, ministered to us by the Divine Spirit who inspired His servant to record them? May we read the Gospels thus? Or is all this but an exquisite dream from which we must awake to the clear, cold light of nineteenth-century criticism?

Chapter 3

In this enlightened age we are not content with checking the spread of a disease when it appears: we seek to diagnose it and to discover its origin. And an inquiry of this kind respecting the prevailing epidemic of unbelief cannot fail to be useful.

The skepticism of the day may be clearly traced to the rationalism which almost swamped the religious life of Germany in the second half of the eighteenth century. But the chief cause of that apostasy has never been fully recognized. Not even in the darkest periods of the history of Christendom had the character and authority of the Bible ever been questioned.[1] It was always regarded as the inspired word of God, the supreme and infallible guide in all questions of faith and morals. But just as apostate Jews in a preceding age had "made the word of God of none effect by their traditions," so also did apostate Christians.

> 1] Questioned by Christians, I mean; and speaking broadly.

In England the law is supreme. But it does not rest with "the man in the street" to interpret the law: that is the function of the King's Courts. And so here. The supremacy of the Bible was unquestioned. But the Church was the "keeper" and the "interpreter" of it; and it so kept it as to keep it from the people, and it so interpreted it as to "change the truth of God into a lie." An open Bible was the prize at stake in the glorious Reformation struggle. The leaders in that great revolt proclaimed the truth of salvation in Christ apart from the Church, and without the intervention of priests. And this truth set the conscience free from the bondage which had enthralled it.

But justification by faith was not the only truth that had been lost in the superstitions of a thousand years. Every truth of the Bible had been perverted or darkened. And yet the men who came after the

Reformers were content to maintain the ground already gained. "The Bible the religion of Protestants" was a proverb in the Reformation age. But in the age which followed it, the religion of Protestants became narrowed to the special truths which the Reformation brought to light. And with what result? In course of time the memory grew dim of the darkness and perils of pre-Reformation times, and of the struggle by which liberty was won. More than this, the methods of the Reformers were forgotten, and the spirit which inspired them had died out. And so it came to pass that when the eighteenth century gave a new impetus to the mental activity and free thought promoted by the Reformation; and the German mind, so famed for its analytical subtlety, turned to the study of Scripture in the cold light of reason, difficulties innumerable presented themselves. And to these difficulties the Evangelical Churches had no adequate answer to offer. The Bible was discredited by the ignorance and incapacity of its defenders; and the resulting mischief has never been retrieved.

It is no reproach upon the Reformers that their writings fail to help us in such bloodless conflicts. For theirs was a life and death struggle such as leaves no leisure for questions like those which make up the stock-in-trade of the critics. But if they could revisit the scenes of their labors and their triumphs, how deep would be their indignation and distress at the discovery that the mass even of real Christians have no fuller knowledge of Divine truth than they themselves had attained. And this wholly understates the case. From the great truths which Luther taught with a fullness and boldness never since surpassed, the Lutheran Churches have largely apostatized. The doctrines of Grace have been swamped in a pagan sacramentalism which destroys true Christianity.

And such an apostasy can only be explained by ignorance of Scripture as a whole. It was charged upon the Hebrew Christians of apostolic days that they were ignorant of the A B C of revealed religion; [1] and a like charge can be sustained against the Evangelicalism of Germany at the close of the eighteenth century. "Truth is one"; but when the circle of Divine truth is broken, men soon forget its unity, and the segments that remain lie open to attack. What advance had been made in the knowledge of Scripture during the two centuries and a half from the date of the Diet of Worms? The Bible as a whole is, of course, "a book of piety"; and its worth in that respect is unchallenged. But, ignoring that element, the Old Testament naturally admits of a threefold division —the historical, the typical, and the prophetical.

> 1] Heb. 5:12.

But history lies outside the special province of theology. Prophecy was ostentatiously neglected until Hengstenberg appealed to its testimony in answering the rationalists. And as for the third division, Hengstenberg himself lamented the prevailing ignorance respecting it. "The elucidation of the doctrine of the types," he declared, "now entirely neglected, is an important problem for future theologians."

And how can anyone who is ignorant of "the doctrine of the types," and of the grand scheme of Divine prophecy, understand the New Testament aright? Such a man has not learned even the language in which the New Testament is written. Nor does this remark apply only to special passages: it bears upon the scope and meaning of entire books, and the relation of the books to one another—the "hidden harmony" of Scripture as a whole.

The rationalistic crusade against the Bible, which Eichhorn christened "the Higher Criticism," owed its strength and success to the appeal it made to the human element in the Scriptures. The Bible is called "the word of God" for the same reason that Christ is called "the Word of God"—it expresses the mind of God. But as Christ is "very God" and yet perfect man, so the Bible, while absolutely Divine, is yet the most human book in all the world. And as the Living Word became subject to all the infirmities of humanity, sin excepted, so also the written Word is marked by all the characteristics of human writings, error excepted.[1] German Evangelicalism, however, had neglected the human side of the Bible, as indeed a certain type of Evangelicalism does to the present day.

> 1] I here use the word "error" in its deeper sense, and I do not prejudge questions which shall be considered in the sequel.

But to attempt to stifle criticism of Scripture by the cry that "the Bible is the word of God" only serves to excite distrust on the part of earnest and honest-hearted inquirers. There never was an attack made upon the truth that could not be refuted. "Truth is one "; but error is in its very nature inconsistent, and therefore absurd. And while Divine truth is spiritual, and can only be spiritually discerned, human error is natural, and can be met on its own ground. We cannot "reason" men into the kingdom of God, but by reasoning we can expose errors which prejudice them against it.

We can appeal to them, moreover, not to expend all their skepticism upon "the Biblical writers," but to reserve a little of it for the critics themselves—to carry the Higher Criticism one step further, and bring the exponents of the science within its scope. Take Professor Blank, for example, who criticizes the Bible in such a patronizing way. Surely it is legitimate to investigate his fitness for his self-appointed task. His eminence as a scholar in his own particular line is unquestioned. But would those who know him best accept him as an arbitrator in any case where a sound judgment, and breadth of view, and common sense are necessary qualifications? Or if the case came into court, and Professor Blank were found to be foreman of the jury empaneled to try it, would not the parties ask for half an hour's adjournment, and retire to consider a compromise rather than go to trial? [1]

> 1] Some years ago I published a defense of one book of Scripture against the attack of an eminent critic, and Mr. Gladstone was at the pains of writing two successive letters to impress on me that the distinguished scholar in question was wholly wanting in the judgment requisite for dealing with questions of the kind.
>
> One of the prominent figures in Charles Lever's most popular novel is Dr. Barrett, who was Vice-Provost of Trinity College, Dublin, a century ago. His extraordinary erudition made him the envy and admiration of contemporary scholars; his extraordinary silliness made him the butt of every undergraduate. And stories of his great learning and his great folly are rife to the present day. And in no department of scholarship is this phenomenon more likely to be manifested than in that of Philology.

"After all," says Matthew Arnold, "shut a number of men up to make study and learning the business of their lives, and how many of them, from want of some discipline or other, seem to lose all balance of judgment, all common sense!" In the same connection, he speaks of "the ordeal of the Englishman's strong and strict sense for fact," and he adds, "We are much mistaken if it does not turn out that this ordeal makes great havoc among the vigorous and rigorous theories of German criticism concerning the Bible-documents." And "German criticism" does not cease to be German because during the present generation it has been fathered by Englishmen.

"Great men are not always wise," [1] and even in the natural sphere they may prove to be blind guides. The "Ptolemaic System" is a monumental proof of this. Pythagoras had taught men to regard the sun as the center of our system; and that truth held sway until, by methods analogous to those of the Higher Critics of today, Ptolemy persuaded his contemporaries to abandon it. And for long centuries all the wisdom of the wise was on the side of error. And when we turn to the religious sphere the wonder is how any Protestant, with the history of Christendom open to him, can be influenced by the dicta of men of intellect and genius. Down to the present hour, have not men of the highest eminence in every branch of human knowledge bartered the truths of Christianity for the pagan superstitions which are the stock-in-trade of priestcraft?

1] Job 32:9.

The leaders in this Higher Criticism crusade in England have facile pens and they are prolific authors. And yet if they may be judged by their writings, there is not one of them who is a student of prophetic truth or of the typology of Scripture. Their Bible is but an ill-assorted collection of Jewish books. Their "Jesus" came to found a new religion, and they seem very hazy about His coming back again. The ground-plan of the Bible they know nothing of.

"The whole Scriptures are a testimony to Christ: the whole history of the chosen people, with its types, and its law, and its prophecies, is a showing forth of Him." Thus wrote Dean Alford, one of the greatest commentators of our age. But all this has no existence for the critics; and if they would speak out plainly, some of them would brand it as superstitious drivel.

As the spiritual Christian reads their books he is conscious of an atmosphere and an environment that are uncongenial. For their writings are in great measure but a post mortem upon dead truth. Some of them, like the Jews of old, have "a zeal for God, but not according to knowledge." But these are a minority. As for the rest, if they have ever known what it means—but here I tread on delicate ground, and I will call a witness from the grave to express my meaning. The following letter, which appeared many years ago in the columns of the Record newspaper, made a profound impression on me at the time, and it may appeal to others today. The writer of it withheld his name, but I was told at the time that he was Professor Birks, of Cambridge. Here are his words:—

> "You well observe in a recent article that the public is becoming accustomed to the strange vagaries on the Bible which men of learning and high position in the Church seem so constantly falling into.
>
> "I should be glad to express, through the medium of your columns, what appears to me the secret of all this; and I the rather desire to do so, because I am myself a monument of the delivering power and mercy of God in this very matter.
>
> "It is very observable that almost all the men who have thus notoriously erred from the way of truth are men of some kind of eminence in natural ability. Of Mr. Maurice I cannot say I think that even in natural things he excels in distinctness of ideas, or the power of clearly discerning nice differences. But the errors of such men as Heath, and especially Bishop Colenso, cannot be attributed to any confusion of mind as to things which differ—their eminent honors at Cambridge forbid our taking that view. Besides, I know from past experience in the same gloomy school, that the possession of very considerable natural acumen does not in the least degree aid a man whose mind is perplexed about the foundations of Bible truth.
>
> "As to the objections urged by the above gentlemen to the generally-received views of Scripture, and the doctrines which flow so immediately from its simple and spiritual acceptance as the Word of God, they know as well as we do that they are hackneyed and as old as our fallen nature, but then that does not remove them; they cannot receive the simple accounts of Scripture, because they have not Divine faith. I remember when I first began to read the Bible (and I thought I was sincerely seeking the truth) I was miserable because I could not believe it; I dared not reject any statement I found there, but I could not fully believe it was true. The Bishop of Natal just expresses what I felt, and the fact that we took exactly the

same University honors (in different years of course) makes me sympathize with him peculiarly. My own history was just this: —I had read and studied deeply in mathematics, had mastered every fresh subject I entered upon with ease and delight; had become accustomed (as every exact mathematician must do) to investigate and discover fundamental differences between things which seem to the uninitiated one and the same; had seen my way into physical astronomy and the higher parts of Newton's immortal 'Principia,' and been frequently lost in admiration of his genius till St. Mary's clock warned me that midnight was past three hours ago. I had, in fact (as we say), made myself master of dynamics, and become gradually more and more a believer in the unlimited capabilities of my own mind! This self-conceited idea was only flattered and fostered by eminent success in the Senate House, and by subsequently obtaining a Fellowship at Trinity, and enjoying very considerable popularity as a mathematical lecturer.

"It would have spared me many an hour of misery in after days had I really felt what I so often said, viz., that the deeper a man went in science, the humbler he ought to be, and the more cautious in pronouncing an independent opinion on a subject he had not investigated or could not thoroughly sift. But, though all this was true, I had yet to learn that this humility in spiritual things is never found in a natural man.

"I took orders, and began to preach, and then, like the Bishop among the Zulus, I found out the grand deficit in my theology. I had not the Spirit's teaching myself, and how could I without it speak "in demonstration of the Spirit and of power"?

"In vain did I read Chalmers, Paley, Butler, Gaussen, etc., and determine that, as I had mastered all the other subjects I had grappled with, so I would the Bible, and that I would make myself a believer. I found a poor, ignorant old woman in my parish more than a match for me in Divine things. I was distressed to find that she was often happy in the evident mercy of the Lord to her, and that she found prayer answered, and that all this was proved sincere by her blameless and harmless walk amongst her neighbors; whilst I, with all my science and investigation, was barren, and unprofitable, and miserable—an unbeliever in heart, and yet not daring to avow it, partly from the fear of man, but more from a certain inward conviction that all my skeptical difficulties would be crushed and leaped over by the experience of the most illiterate Christian.

"I was perfectly ashamed to feel in my mind like Voltaire, Volney, or Tom Paine. I could claim no originality for my views; and I found they were no comfort, but a constant source of misery to me.

"It may now be asked how I came ever to view Divine truth differently. I desire to ascribe all praise to Him to whom power belongeth; I desire to put my own mouth in the dust, and be ashamed, and never open my mouth anymore, because of my former unbelief. I cannot describe all I passed through, but I desire with humility and gratitude to say, I was made willing in a day of Christ's power. He melted down my proud heart with His love; He shut my mouth forever from cavilling at any difficulties in the written Word; and one of the first things in which the great change appeared was, that whereas beforetime preaching had been misery, now it became my delight to be able to say, without a host of skeptical or infidel doubts rushing into my mind, 'Thus saith the Lord.' Oh, I am quite certain no natural man can see the things of God; and I am equally certain he cannot make himself do so. 'It was the Lord that exalted Moses and Aaron,' said Samuel; and, 'By the grace of God I am what I am,' said St Paul; and so, in a modified and humble sense, I can truly say.

"It used to be a terrible stumbling-block to me to find so many learned men, so many acute men, so many scientific men, infidels. It is not so now; I see that God has said,' Not many wise men after the flesh, not many mighty, not many noble'; I see, as plainly as it is possible for me to see anything, that no natural man can receive the things of the Spirit of God. Hence I expect to find men of this stamp of intellect coming out boldly with their avowals of unbelief in the written Word of God. The only answer I can give to them is: 'God has in mercy taught me better'; and never do I sing those beautiful words in the well-known hymn but I feel my eyes filling with tears of gratitude to the God of all compassion—

> "Jesus sought me when a stranger,
> Wandering from the fold of God."

"So it was with me; so it must be with any one of them if ever they are to know the truth in its power, or to receive the love of the truth that they may be saved.

"I feel very much for the young of this generation, remembering the conflicts I passed through in consequence of the errors of men of ability." [1]

> 1] After the Third Edition of this book had gone to press, the author ascertained that the writer of the foregoing letter (which appeared in the Record, October, 1862) was the Rev. Robert Walker, M.A., Vicar of Wymeswold, Leicestershire.

Chapter 4

I have always felt that the death of Charles II. left a stain upon the fair fame of England. No, I do not mean Charles I; neither would I endorse the words of Junius that "he ought to have died upon the same scaffold." For that Whitehall execution is a matter as to which opinions may differ. But that the nation that beheaded his father and deposed his brother should have permitted him, after such a reign, to die in his Palace as King of England—this is a fact which in my humble judgment is discreditable to the English people.

Even during that infamous reign there were multitudes of people who believed in the virtue of women. But no person of culture—no one who was abreast of the times, or who understood the trend of contemporary thought — acknowledged a traditional belief of that kind. And "Society" tacitly ignored it. In fact it came to be looked upon as proof of narrow-mindedness or boorishness. The profession of morality became unfashionable. The standard of morality was. gone.

The analogy between faith and morals is close and real. And the decline of morality in the Restoration period is finding its counterpart in the sphere of faith today. We have come within sight of an apostasy unparalleled in the history of Christendom. Every attack which open infidelity has ever launched against the Bible is now being repeated by men "who profess and call themselves Christians," and who claim to be the apostles of a new movement in defense of the citadel of Christian truth. And just as vice became fashionable in the days of Charles II., so, as Professor Cheyne naively owns, this system of attacking truth in the interests of truth has become "fashionable" in Britain today. The appearance of his Encyclopedia has checked the movement for the moment: but the scare thus caused will soon subside. It has fluttered the lesser lights of the Higher Criticism, who have been serving as acolytes in the worship of this new goddess of Reason. For they are not clear-headed enough to see that Professor Cheyne has only pressed their own principles to legitimate conclusions. Without help from France, Charles II. could not so easily have overcome what he deemed English prudery; and so here, foreign critics have been called in to force the pace with their British brethren. The French women were more "advanced" than the English; that was all. And this is precisely what is said about the Encyclopedia writers as compared with ordinary British critics.

The late Professor Robertson Smith is appealed to on every hand in proof that there is nothing in the Higher Criticism to injure or alarm a Christian. By far the most interesting personality among contemporary critics, his apologia, published soon after he was deprived of his Chair in Aberdeen, was marked by the glow of real spirituality. Evangelical fervor, too, characterized the man. As honest and upright as he was amiable and attractive, he seemed at that time to be a martyr to the cause of truth. It is this very element, however, that makes his case such a warning.

"Thanks to the cold sluggishness of our national character," well - seasoned "society ladies" may possibly have spent a dozen years at the court of Charles without becoming much worse than when they entered it. But no pure woman in the gush and glow of life could pass through such an ordeal without sinking to the level of those by whom she was surrounded. And no man of Robertson Smith's temperament could allow his mind year after year to be saturated with German infidelity, and yet end where he began. His Old Testament in the Jewish Church discloses what he was in 1881: the *Encyclopedia Biblica* shows what he became. For by him it was that this sad book "was originated." He it was "who requested Professor Cheyne to take up the work as showing his own 'uncompromisingly progressive spirit.'" [1]

1] The Times, April 11, 1902.

People are led to suppose that the Higher Criticism is the outcome of an honest inquiry after truth. But the history of the movement as written by the critics themselves explodes such a delusion. [1] Of Eichhorn, "the founder of modern Old Testament criticism," Professor Cheyne writes that "it was his hope to contribute to the winning back of the educated classes to religion." And to attain this end he set himself to eliminate from the Bible everything to which the rationalists took exception. "Religion" is fair ground for compromise; but Christianity is not a religion but a faith; and faith, like morality, admits of no compromise.

> 1] In proof of my words I need but appeal to Professor Cheyne's *Founders of Old Testament Criticism.*

Men like Matthew Arnold may create a mythical "Jesus" out of materials supplied by an expurgated edition of the Gospels, from which everything distasteful to their fastidious skepticism has been eliminated. And they may make this "Jesus" the Buddha of an ideal religion which will please everyone except the sinner who is conscious of his need of a Divine Savior. But all this is treason to the Christ of God; and the Christian who sets himself to "huckster" [1] the truth in this way, either sinks to the level of the rationalist, or leads others down to that abyss. This may take two generations to accomplish. Eichhorn's greatest pupil, Ewald, was as devout as himself, but his criticisms were more searching. Ewald's greatest pupil, Wellhausen, became a mere rationalist; and, as Professor Cheyne justly says, he only applied Ewald's principles more consistently. [2]

> 1] 2 Cor. 2:17. The primary meaning of the word translated "to corrupt" is "to huckster," and the whole passage indicates that it is in this sense the apostle uses it. Eichhorn treated the Bible on the principle of a "Dutch auction"; he adapted his wares to the market, huckstering the Scriptures to suit the rationalists.
>
> 2] *Founders of Old Testament Criticism*, p. 107.

Professor Cheyne himself is the English Wellhausen. [1] He is our only critic of eminence who is clear-sighted enough to see the end of the road on which he is travelling, or courageous enough to follow it. In his judgment, expressed of course in veiled language and with perfect courtesy, other critics, such for example as his distinguished colleague at Oxford, are the timid advocates of an impossible compromise. Professor Driver's "sympathy with old-fashioned readers" has led him, he says, "to forget the claims of criticism." [2] It is this "spirit of compromise" [3] that Professor Cheyne "chiefly dreads." And the compromise he deprecates is not Eichhorn's compromise with rationalists, but the tendency of the English critics to pander to the weakness of those who revere the Bible and believe in the Divinity of Christ. We have already seen how summarily he rejects the foundations of Christianity, and we need not be surprised at his assertion that by no one "has it yet been made probable that there was a historical individual among the ancestors of the Israelites called Abram." [4] The existence of Abraham is not even probable. The skeptic would say it is not "certain," and thus leave an opening for discussion; but on both vital and incidental questions Professor Cheyne has the courage of his convictions, and boldly takes the unassailable ground of open infidelity. [5]

> 1] Only in the sense here indicated. For unlike Wellhausen, Professor Cheyne is always reverent in tone, and he is one of the fairest of the critics.
>
> 2] *Founders of Old Testament Criticism*, p. 366.
>
> 3] Ibid., p. 247.
>
> 4] Founders of Old Testament Criticism, p. 239.
>
> 5] Infidelity is a strong term, but not too strong. In an article in *The Nineteenth Century* for January, 1902, Professor Cheyne says that Abraham was a "lunar hero." Having regard to our Lord's references to the Patriarch, this is shockingly profane; and having regard to the recent discoveries of archaeology, it is on other grounds extraordinary. Professor Cheyne would possibly deny that he says this. But he says that Winckler, the German, says it; and he repeats it with approval, calling it "A turning-point in Old Testament study," and commending it to the attention of English scholars. I never knew a receiver of stolen goods who did not resent being called a thief!

Here I would wish to expose another popular blunder. The idea prevails that the Higher Criticism is the special preserve of Hebrew scholars. Now this is undoubtedly true of the sort of study for which Eichhorn coined the title, namely, a critical examination of the text of a book with a view to analyzing its contents. But anyone can see that there is no connection whatsoever between an inquiry of that kind and the rejection of the supernatural element in the Bible in order to propitiate the Rationalists. We must avoid the stupid pedantry of explaining a phrase by its origin and not by its use. The Higher Criticism at once degenerated into what it is today a skeptical crusade against the Bible, tending to lower it to the level of a purely human book.

Here, however, the pioneers of criticism compare favorably with their successors. They had the excuse of the ignorance which then prevailed about Old Testament times. The attack on the Pentateuch, for example, was based on the assumption that the Mosaic Era was a barbarous age. It seemed an anachronism to suppose that such a literature could have existed at such a time. But this, as Professor Sayce will tell us, was "a baseless assumption due to the ignorance of the critic." [1] Referring to the work of "the excavator and the decipherer" in Eastern lands, the same writer goes on to say, "Discovery has followed there upon discovery, each more marvelous than the last, and a lost world of culture and civilization has been brought to light. . . . We can follow the daily life of the Egyptian 3,000 years ago more minutely than the daily life of a mediaeval Englishman; . and study the letters of Canaanites who lived before the birth of Moses." And again, "In the century before the Exodus, Palestine was a land of books and schools." [2]

1] *Lex Mosaica*, p. 7.
2] *Lex Mosaica*, p. 9.

But though the only reasonable foundation of the attack on the Pentateuch has thus been destroyed, the critics go on repeating the statements made in ignorance of all this by their great predecessors. Or if they try to shore up their crumbling edifice, it is by the abuse of a few isolated texts which are pressed remorselessly into the service. [1]

1] See Appendix, Note I.

Let this fact, then, be kept prominently in view, that a knowledge of Hebrew has nothing whatever to do with the question of the authenticity of the books of Moses. And speaking generally, philology has only an incidental importance in the whole Higher Criticism controversy. If, for example, Professor Driver declares that "the Hebrew of Daniel is that of a much later age than the sixth century B.C.," he is answered by Professor Cheyne, who, though a more uncompromising critic, is a safer guide on matters of this kind. We may therefore dismiss the Hebraists altogether from this part of the inquiry. And even in relation to questions which specially concern them, the function of the experts is merely to prepare the proofs. The decision should rest with those who have practical experience in dealing with evidence. To allow the critics to adjudicate upon the evidence they have themselves prepared would be quite as stupid and as dangerous as to permit the police to try the prisoners whose cases they bring into court. And yet this is, speaking generally, the attitude maintained by educated Englishmen towards every question raised in this controversy. It is intellectually as deplorable as that of the Irish Roman Catholic peasant who grovels before his priest and takes the law from his mouth.

Take for example the Isaiah controversy. The critical attack upon Daniel not only destroys one of the great Messianic prophecies, and impairs the authority of the New Testament, but impugns the teaching of the Lord Himself. But this "second Isaiah" hypothesis involves no element of this kind. The question therefore is open to discussion, and the Christian may consider it on its merits. The reasons urged in favor of it are undoubtedly striking and important. They are, first, certain literary differences which mark the various sections of the Book; and secondly, the definiteness of the references to the exile and the return, contained in the latter portion of it. No one will dispute, however, that were it not for this second consideration the question would not be pressed; for in a writer so "versatile" as Isaiah, [1] a change of style is by no means extraordinary. And the critics do not deny that God might have inspired Isaiah to utter all these prophecies.

> 1] "A writer so versatile and dramatic." Professor G. A. Smith's Isaiah.

In a recent sensational murder trial, it was suggested that the real delinquent was a stranger who resembled the accused. The suggestion was a reasonable one, and its acceptance would have explained certain difficulties in the case for the prosecution. But an experienced judge and a sensible jury wanted to know where this stranger had come from, and what became of him. And so here. We want to know something about this Isaiah II. [1]

> 1] I fear I shall be deemed ignorant for speaking of two Isaiahs. I really forget how many of them are reckoned by some of the critics—sixteen, I think. But in these pages I wish to deal seriously with the criticisms of sober scholars, and to ignore the vagaries of faddists.

If it were possible to hold that the "second Isaiah" was the real Isaiah, this difficulty might perhaps be ignored. For the author of the opening prophecies of the Book— those scathing denunciations of the religion of the people—may well have been hated and persecuted; and it is conceivable that his very name should have been erased from the popular annals. But the last twenty-seven chapters are altogether unique, not merely by reason of their unequalled brilliancy and power, but also because they are such "comfortable words" as never before or since were heard in Israel. A prophet raised up in the dark days of the exile to deliver such messages of hope and joy would have become immortal. He would have been the idol of the whole nation, the most famous and popular personage of his time. But if we are to accept the theory of the critics, he appeared and vanished again, like a morning mist, without leaving even the vaguest tradition of his name, his personality, or his career. And this, remember, in the exilic or post-exilic period, that is to say within historic times.

And when we are told that there were several "second Isaiahs," a galaxy of the most brilliant prophetic stars that ever shone in the national firmament of Israel, the suggestion becomes so utterly preposterous that if the case could be brought before any serious judicial tribunal it would be "laughed out of court."

But as usual with experts, the critics look only at one side of the question. And while experience refuses to sanction an hypothesis so wild as that which they propose, it warns us authoritatively that in common with all experts they are exceptionally liable to err.

In his *History of the Criminal Law*, Sir James Fitzjames Stephens places on record the matured judgment of the Judicial Bench that no kind of evidence needs more the test of cross-examination than that of experts. In no other sphere save that of religious controversy would sensible people accept the dicta of experts until they had been thus tested; and yet the history of the Higher Criticism movement gives abundant proof that no class of expert is more untrustworthy than the critic.

What about Schleiermacher, and Baur, and Strauss, and their several schools? Who now defends their conclusions? The New Testament fared worse at their hands than does the Old Testament today at the hands of their successors. And yet the lucubrations of those brilliant scholars and critics are now put aside as "an episode" even by such an arch-heretic as Professor Harnack of Berlin. "There was a time" (he writes) "—the general public indeed have not got beyond it—in which the oldest Christian literature, including the New Testament, was looked upon as a tissue of deceptions and forgeries. That time is passed. For science it was an episode in which it learned much, and after which it has much to forget. . . . The oldest literature of the Church in all main points and in most details, from the point of view of literary criticism, is genuine and trustworthy." [1]

> 1] He adds: "In the whole New Testament there is in all probability only a single writing which can be looked upon as pseudonymous in the strictest sense of the word—i.e., 2 Peter."

What guarantee have we, then, that the vagaries of present-day criticism about the Books of Moses, the Prophets and the Psalms, will not be dismissed as lightly by the Higher Critics of the future? I am not referring here to the puerilities of "the Polychrome Bible" — such puerilities offend the common sense of all intelligent people. What I have in view is such theories, for example, as that the dispensation of the prophets preceded the dispensation of the law—a very slight acquaintance with the general scheme of revelation will save us from any error of the kind; or to take another case, that prophetic writings which deal with the events of the captivity must be assigned to the captivity era. This theory originated with the skeptics, and it is a necessary part of the rationalistic crusade against the supernatural element in Scripture. But it is adopted by critics of a different school, who defend it on the ground that to suppose a prophet to become "immersed in the future would be not only without parallel in the Old Testament, it would be contrary to the nature of prophecy." [1]

1] Professor Driver's Introduction, p. 224.

Now this is a question as to which we need no help from the philologist. Any Christian who has made a life study of the Bible is as competent to form an opinion upon it as the ablest Hebraist in Christendom. And most of us would insist that this theory is utterly opposed to fact. If the 64th chapter of Isaiah was necessarily written after the captivity, the 53rd chapter was necessarily written after the crucifixion. And so also with the Messianic Psalms, and numberless passages in the minor prophets. Professor Driver tells us that "the prophet never abandons his own historical position." And therefore he calls the prophecies of Isaiah "discourses." In other words, the prophecies came by the will of man. But no prophecy of the Scripture is of this character. "For no prophecy ever came by the will of man; but men spake from God, being moved by the Holy Ghost"—borne along as a storm-caught ship is driven before the wind. [1]

> 1] 2 Peter 1:21. The word "moved" is literally carried along: see its use in Acts xxvii. 15, 17 (driven). The whole passage is of great importance in this connection—" No prophecy of the Scripture is of any private interpretation." The word rendered "interpretation" occurs here only. The verb is used in the LXX. (Gen. xli. 12) as the translation of the Hebrew pathar, to open unfold, disclose. And the word here rendered "private" occurs 113 times in the New Testament, but nowhere else is it so translated. It is rendered "his own" 77 times. And the word "is" is not the verb to be, but to come into existence, to come to be. What the passage declares, therefore, is that no prophecy ever originated with the prophet's own unfolding (or sending forth). It speaks, not of the interpretation of the prophecies, but of their origin and source, and thus disposes of the theories of the critics. (See Dr. Bullinger's *Figures of Speech used in the Bible*, p. 130.)

Chapter 5

Charles Reade, the great novelist, thus states in his own inimitable way the attitude of the Christianized skeptic toward the miraculous in Scripture: "Say there never was a miracle and never will be, and I differ with, but cannot confute you. Deny the creation and the possibility of a re-creation or resurrection; call David a fool for saying, 'It is He that hath made us and not we ourselves,' and a wise man for suggesting that, on the contrary, molecules created themselves without a miracle, and we made ourselves out of molecules without a miracle; and although your theory contradicts experience as much as, and staggers credulity more than, any miracle that has ever been ascribed by Christians or Jews to infinite power, I admit it is consistent, though droll."

But, he goes on to say, once grant the creation of the world, and "it is a little too childish to draw back" and to haggle over miracles of the kind recorded in the Bible.

The intelligent and consistent skeptic is entitled to respect and sympathy. But what can be said for the man who professes to believe in the Apostles' Creed, and yet rejects on *a priori* grounds the Gospel miracles!

Here is the preface to the Fourth Gospel: — "In the beginning was the Word, and the Word was with God, and the Word was God. The same was in the beginning with God. All things were made by Him; and without Him was not anything made that was made." The skeptic at once declares his unbelief. And from his own standpoint he is right; for he regards the record as human, and no one but a credulous fool would believe such statements on merely human authority. The Christianized skeptic, on the other hand, assures us that "the Nazarene" was really the God who made the heavens and the earth; and yet he cannot believe in His healing a case of paralysis, or raising Lazarus from the dead. [1] Was there ever such an instance of "straining out a gnat and swallowing a camel"!

1] John 5:1-9; 11:44.

For not only do the minor and incidental miracles of the Ministry rest upon the same testimony as the great foundation miracle of the Incarnation, but if that greatest of the miracles be accepted, the others are in such sense connected with it that, even if no record of them remained, we might reasonably assume they took place. Will my readers decide this question for themselves? Suppose a parent, or wife, or husband, or child were lying at the point of death, and you knew that He who made the world was sojourning in our midst "in fashion as a man," would all the Professors and skeptic s of Christendom prevent you from seeking His presence, and casting yourself at His feet with the appeal that He would cure your loved one?

But it may be said, if this argument were sound such cures would be as frequent now as in the days of the Ministry. To which I answer first, that this objection is not legitimate with the Christian, for the Scriptures themselves explain the mystery of a silent heaven in the present dispensation; and secondly, that notwithstanding that explanation, the silence is the greatest trial which faith has to endure. Matthew Arnold's God — "the Eternal, not ourselves, that makes for righteousness" —may satisfy the student in the dreamland of his library; but men who have to do with the stern realities of life will say of this fastidious skeptic what Pascal said of Descartes, that the only God he admitted was a God who was useless. There are times in every life when "heart and flesh cry out for the Living God" [1] — a real, personal God. Reason revolts against the conception of a God that could not cure our sick, and heal our afflicted ones. His power is beyond question. If, then, He does not do it, are we to conclude that His goodness and love are at fault? This is a part of the searching discipline of the life of faith. [2]

1] Psa. 75:2.

2] *The Silence of God* deals specially with this question.

It is at the foundations that intelligent and true skepticism challenges the truth of Christianity. The miracles controversy is the merest skirmishing. The Divinity of Christ is the field upon which must be fought the decisive battle between faith and unbelief. From the human standpoint, the supreme miracle of the Incarnation is incredible. Here the Christian and the unbeliever measure their distance. And the one as well as the other holds a position which is unassailable. It is the attempted compromise of the Christianized skeptic which is intellectually contemptible. The skeptic says, "No amount of human testimony could avail to accredit such a miracle; therefore I reject it." The Christian leaves that position unchallenged, but he answers, "The truth you refuse does not rest upon human testimony, but upon a Divine revelation; therefore I accept it."

Let me repeat my question in another form. And here I appeal to any honest, sane, and sensible man, I care not whether he be believer or unbeliever, Christian or Pagan: Suppose the Divine Being who made heaven and earth were sojourning among us, would you expect Him to work what we call miracles? In other words, would you attribute to Him power greater than we ourselves possess? The question needs only to be stated; for the answer is obvious. Not only should we look for miracles, but if, in circumstances which would lead any good man to act, the miracles were wanting, their absence would discredit the assumption that the Being was Divine.

The more closely this matter is investigated, the more clearly it will appear that the Divinity of Christ is the pivot on which the whole controversy turns; and the effect of skeptical criticism upon every fearless and logical thinker will be to compel him to make choice "between a deeper faith and a bolder unbelief."

Says Matthew Arnold, "At the stage of experience where men have now arrived, it is evident to whoever looks at things fairly that the miraculous data of the Bible . . . proceed from a medium of imperfect observation and boundless credulity. The story of the miraculous birth and resuscitation of Jesus was bred in such a medium." [1] I respect a thinker and writer of this type, and I freely acknowledge that if the Bible be nothing more than these Higher Critics would have us believe, he is entirely in the right. The Christian believes, while the skeptic rejects, "the story of the miraculous birth." But the Christianized skeptic s accept the Christian's creed while they destroy the foundation on which it rests. And yet they pose as persons of superior enlightenment and intelligence!

> 1] God and the Bible (Preface). His argument against the evidential value of miracles (*Lit. and Dogma*, chap. 6 especially) I deal with in my Silence of God, though without

citing him. With much of it I agree. The assumption that miracles are impossible indicates merely the stupid tendency of the human mind to become enslaved to the results of experience. It reminds me of Dean Swift's story of the man with the wonderful nose. The learned society of the place met to discuss the case, and passed a resolution that no man could have such a nose. At which juncture the man himself walked in, nose and all! Anyone can find proofs that what are called miracles occur even in our own day.

If people would use their reason and common sense in this matter, the battle would soon be joined between faith and unbelief, and we should be rid of the shallow and illogical half-skepticism of the critics. A teacher appeared in Judea, and proclaimed himself to be the Son of God and Israel's Messiah. Utterly unaccredited by the established religion of the time, he gathered round him a company of disciples—humble men all of them, mostly peasants and fishermen, wholly unknown to fame. Every element that, in our own day, we should call orthodox and respectable agreed in repudiating him. We are apt to assume that the religious leaders of the Jews were either fools or fiends, whereas the testimony of the Apostle Paul gives proof that they were men of piety and zeal—men who were certainly not inferior in these respects to the religious leaders of Christendom at any period of its history.

But these men rejected Him on perfectly reasonable grounds. It is, perhaps, impossible for us to understand their position, or to view the facts as they viewed them. But here is the startling testimony of one who in early life had stood where they did. "There was in such a Messiah," he writes, "absolutely nothing—past, present, or possible; intellectually, religiously, or even nationally—to attract, but all to repel." [1]

> 1 Dr. Edersheim, *Life and Times of the Messiah* (vol. 1, p. 145).

How was it, then, that His disciples believed on Him? "Thou art the Christ, the Son of the Living God," was the Apostle Peter's testimony. To which the Lord made answer, "Flesh and blood hath not revealed it unto thee, but my Father which is in heaven." [1] The facts were the same for both. But the facts were regarded from wholly different points of view. The Jews regarded them in the light of human judgment: the disciples viewed them in the light of a Divine revelation.

1] Matt. 26:16, 17.

And the reasons given for disparaging the Bible today are but the echo of the reasons urged for rejecting Christ in the days of the Ministry. One of the popular exponents of the Higher Criticism has denounced the "baseless notion that a book written by human pens and handed down by human methods, transcribed, translated, compiled by fallible minds, is, or can be, the Word of God." Yes; this is so very like what they said about the Lord. "Is not this the carpenter, the son of Mary, the brother of James and Joses and Judas and Simon? And are not His sisters here with us? And" (the record adds) "they were offended at Him." [1] Of course they were; and if the critics, including the writer I have quoted, had lived in the days of the Ministry, their principles would have led them to take sides with those who rejected Him.

1] Mark 6:3.

"But the Bible contains not only what is false, but what is positively immoral and evil." Yes; and they said of Him, "Behold a gluttonous man and a wine-bibber." [1] They even called Him Beelzebub; [2] and the critics have never gone so far as this in denouncing Holy Scripture.

1] Matt. 11:19.

2] Ibid. 10:25.

These grosser charges against the Lord were altogether blasphemous; and so are these baser libels upon the Scriptures. They discredit only those who make them. But as regards what may be described as legitimate criticisms, it will be urged that the critics are fair and intelligent and devout, and that they can prove the truth of all they say. Yes, they think they can prove the truth of it. And many of the leaders of the Jews were quite as devout and intelligent and fair as they. The facts, moreover, on which the Jews relied in denying that the Nazarene could be the Son of God were indisputable; whereas the grounds on which the critics deny that the Bible can be the Word of God are most of them untenable, and all of them disputed. [1] And those that are admitted — the "human pens" and "human methods" — have their counterpart in the facts of the family and workshop at Nazareth.

1] See Chaps. 7, and 8, post.

I am not playing with words. Nor am I using the rejection of Christ as a mere illustration of my theme. This would be irreverent. I insist that the cases are parallel. There is a definite analogy between the grounds on which the Jews rejected Christ and the grounds on which some critics reject the Bible. And the cause of the rejection is the same in both cases—the incapacity of unspiritual men to deal with spiritual things. If the Lord had not claimed to be Divine, they would have ranked Him among the greatest of their Rabbis. And if the Bible did not claim to be Divine, it would be held in the highest honor by many who now disparage it. But the Jews insisted that the Lord should be judged like any other human being, just as the critics maintain that the Bible must be treated like any human book. And the inevitable result in the one case was the crucifixion of Calvary: in the other, it is the apostasy of the *Encyclopedia Biblica*.

That "a book written by human pens, and handed down by human methods," should be the Word of God, does not seem so wild a suggestion as that "the carpenter, the son of Mary," should be the Son of God. As for the book, even if we throw in the "transcribing" and "translating," not only does the notion not appear "baseless" at all, but the objections to it can be shown to be either inapplicable or frivolous. [1]

1] See Chaps. 7, and 8, post.

If positive proof be demanded that the Bible is the Word of God, we must rise above the level at which the critics ply their trade—we must take account of its deeper, spiritual meaning; but in answering their objections and criticisms we can meet the critics on their own ground. Not so with the truth that "the Nazarene" was the Son of God. Here we are confronted with that which not only clashes with all experience, but which transcends all human thought. Therefore it is that flesh and blood cannot reveal it .

And these solemn words of the Lord Jesus Christ are not falsified by the fact that there are multitudes who, apart from any spiritual appreciation of a Divine revelation, profess to believe in His Divinity. For the acceptance of what is true in itself, if it be based on grounds which are either false or inadequate, is not faith but superstition. And of this character are all beliefs begotten of mere "religion," whether the religion be called Christian or Pagan. For, as Pascal wrote, religion makes people stupid. [1]

> 1] The passage is given in God and the Bible (Preface). He is dealing with the difficulty people urge that they cannot believe, and his prescription is that they should act as if they believed; using "the ordinances" —taking holy water, having masses said, &c, and he adds:— *Naturellement mime cela vous fera croire & vous abetira.* No wonder that the Port Royal editors suppressed a passage so cruelly cynical but so true! For while Christianity elevates and ennobles the whole being, mere religion seems to make men either fools or fiends.

Chapter 6

Shifting the burden of proof is one of the commonest tricks of casuistry. By this artifice Infidelity would inveigle us into allowing a presumption against the existence of a written revelation. But, as has been well said, "Agnosticism assumes a double incompetence—the incompetence not only of man to know God, but of God to make Himself known. But the denial of competence is the negation of Deity. For the God who could not speak would not be rational, and the God who would not speak would not be moral." And the author of these words [1] sums up his argument by declaring that "the idea of a written revelation may be said to be logically involved in the notion of a living God."

1] Principal Fairbairn, of Oxford.

This might be stated much more strongly. What should we think of a man who, living in wealth in some distant colony, never communicated with his family in England, even though aware of their being in perplexity and trouble and want? [1] It seems inconceivable that a good and loving God could leave His offspring without a revelation during their sojourn in a world so full of doubt and care and sorrow and sin. But these pages are addressed to Christians, and every Christian believes that we have a revelation. In spite of all that has been said about it, indeed, some of us believe that the Bible is the Word of God. But this only proves our want of intelligence. For, we are assured, no one believes it nowadays unless he is "a brainless idiot." [2]

1] Even among criminals it is only the most degraded of men who forget their families.

2] If the author I quote were living I should pillory him by giving his name. But as he has gone to his account, I abstain from doing so.

Chapter 6

The study of the law, Edmund Burke declares, "does more to quicken and invigorate the understanding than all other kinds of learning put together." Here then is the mature and deliberate testimony of a great lawyer: "Frequent perusals of the Old and New Testament have satisfied him that each is an inspired work, such as no wisdom of man could have framed; and further, that the earlier Revelation is inseparably connected with the later, as the acorn is connected with the oak which springs from it." [1] This "brainless idiot" was Lord Chancellor of England.

1] Lord Hatherley's *Continuity of Scripture.*

Among the other "brainless idiots" who have in the full blaze of modern "culture" cherished this despised belief in the Bible, may be reckoned his immediate successor, Lord Cairns, the greatest Lord Chancellor of modern times. I am assured that Lord Selborne may be classed in the same category. And to them may be added two other very eminent lawyers and judges, Lord Justice Lush and Mr. Justice Archibald. In such company no one need be ashamed of belonging to the guild of the "brainless idiots." And if the faith of the Christian rested on such a basis, it might be shown that that guild includes not a few of the greatest of living scholars and thinkers.

But it is not because the Bible is accredited by the faith of eminent and saintly men that the Christian reverences it as the Word of God. And it is for the Christian I am writing. Were it otherwise, my argument would run on wholly different lines. And if any one demands my definition of a Christian, I may answer, for my present purpose, everyone who accepts the "Apostles' Creed"; everyone who believes that the Lord Jesus Christ was the Only-begotten Son of God. Now the only rational basis for such a belief is a Divine revelation. The man who denies the inspiration of the Gospels, and yet believes in the Incarnation, is, I repeat, a credulous person who would believe anything. With the honest agnostic or infidel I should wish to discuss this question in a patient and sympathetic spirit; but with fools I have neither sympathy nor patience. Here, however, I am addressing neither honest infidels nor credulous fools, but Christians whose faith is being undermined by both.

And the moment we accept the Gospels as a Divine revelation, we have done with that *protégé* of the critics, the "historic Jesus," and we stand in the presence of our Divine Lord and Savior. And from

His hands it is that we receive the Hebrew Scriptures. Three times over in the Temptation He appealed to the Book of Deuteronomy as the Word of God —His only defense and answer to the Devil's arguments and claims. And in the Sermon on the Mount He says: "Think not that I am come to destroy the law or the prophets; I am not come to destroy, but to fulfil. For verily I say unto you, Till heaven and earth pass, one jot or one tittle shall in no wise pass from the law till all be fulfilled." The "jot" is the smallest letter in the alphabet; the "tittle" is one of the smallest strokes—minute points and projections, by which certain letters are distinguished. No language could express more unequivocally the Divine authority of every detail of "the law and the prophets." [1]

> 1] "A book partly legend, partly dishonest legend, fabrications for a purpose, with history which is not history, with a Levitical code made 1000 years after the time of Moses, . . .—can such a book as this be one to which the Son of God puts the solemn declaration above given?"—*Higher Criticism, What is it?* By Rev. Robert Sinker, D.D., of Cambridge, p. 170.

And in His teaching after the resurrection, we are told, "Beginning at Moses and all the prophets, He expounded unto them in all the Scriptures the things concerning Himself." [1] Dean Alford's note upon this is so admirable and so apt, that I cannot refrain from quoting it. The "things concerning Himself," he says, "mean something very different from mere prophetical passages. The whole Scriptures are a testimony to Him: the whole history of the chosen people, with its types, and its law, and its prophecies, is a shewing forth of Him. And it was here the whole that He laid out before them . . . the meaning of the whole, as a whole, fulfilled in Him."

> 1] Luke 24:27.

That this was the Lord's estimate of the Hebrew Scriptures I need not delay to prove. For it is not disputed. The Higher Critics acknowledge it, and as it bars advance in their skeptical crusade against the Bible, they give it prominent notice. To avoid risk of misrepresentation, I always like to state the views of opponents in their own words. So I turn again to the most up-to-date and accredited text-book of the Higher Criticism. And here I read: "Both Christ and the apostles or writers of the New Testament held the current Jewish notions respecting the Divine authority and revelation of the Old Testament." [1]

> 1] Hastings' *Bible Dictionary*, article "Old Testament," p. 601.

How inferior the Christ of these critics is to themselves, both in spiritual and natural intelligence! But the profanity of the words, and the folly and conceit which they betoken, will be plain to every Christian. What the decoy is to the libertine, these men are, though unwittingly, to the avowed infidel. Just as a pure woman is insidiously trained to hear language and to tolerate suggestions which in time prepare the way for advances of a kind that at first would have excited disgust and anger; so the holy and healthy spiritual instincts of the Christian are gradually deadened by his becoming accustomed to hear his Divine Lord thus patronized and disparaged.

"Writings of this character are far more dangerous to the simple-minded Christian than any direct attack on his Master. They are very shockingly irreverent. A patronizing tone is assumed, which exhibits the critic as presuming to judge Him who, we believe, will be our Judge." These weighty words, which the Christian will do well to ponder, are from the pen of one of the Lord Chancellors whom I have already quoted.

If the subject were not too sad and too solemn for ridicule, I would illustrate this teaching by applying it in another sphere. Why should not a man have two wives?

The question will provoke a wild scream of indignation: in view of the teaching of the New Testament, how can anyone dare to raise it? Yes, the teaching of the New Testament is explicit, but "both Christ and the apostles or writers of the New Testament held the current Jewish notions respecting" marriage. The importance of the question of marriage is absolutely trivial in comparison with that of the character and authority of Holy Scripture. And if the testimony of the Gospels and Epistles on the one question may be thus evaded, it is mere trifling to appeal to it on the other. If the Higher Critics' estimate of the Bible be a just one, then, in view of the history of the Patriarchs, the position of woman and the sacredness of marriage must be classed with the superstitions which the Christian religion has borrowed from a degenerate Judaism.

Most true it is that the Lord Jesus Christ was man, and that "being found in fashion as a man He humbled Himself." Within certain limits therefore, Kenosis [1] theories have their place. But not upon the question here at issue. To assert that His teaching had no higher authority than that of man, is a perilous position for a Christian to assume. But even if we could for the sake of argument concede this, it would not touch the fact that the same Holy Spirit who inspired mere men to speak from God, was given to Him without measure; and on that Divine fact He based His claim to speak "the words of God." [2]

> 1] A Greek word, the noun of the verb used in Phil. 2:7. ("He emptied Himself," R.V.)
>
> 2] John 3:34.

What mean such statements as these, "He that rejecteth Me and receiveth not My words hath one that judgeth him: the word that I have spoken, the same shall judge him in the last day. For I have not spoken of Myself; but the Father which sent me, He gave me a commandment, what I should say, and what I should speak." [1] And again, "Believest thou not that I am in the Father, and the Father in Me? The words that I speak unto you, I speak not of Myself." [2] In view of such language, we can understand His solemn declaration, "Heaven and earth shall pass away, but My words shall not pass away." [3]

> 1] John 12:48, 49.
>
> 2] Ibid. 14:10.
>
> 3] Luke 21:33.

"The Word was made flesh and dwelt among us, full of grace and truth" — not grace only, but TRUTH; for "grace and truth came by Jesus Christ." [1] Hence His testimony to Himself, "I am the light of the world;" [2] "I am the way, the truth, and the life." [3] And yet we are told deliberately by men who claim to be Christians and Christian ministers, that His whole teaching respecting matters of vital importance in relation to faith and morals, was steeped in ignorance and superstition. For let the facts be kept clearly in view: we are called "brainless idiots" for believing that the Old Testament is the Word of God; and yet in this we are merely following our Divine Lord.

1] John 1:14, 17. 5

2] Ibid 8:12.

3] Ibid 14:6.

It is not easy to write calmly upon this subject, but I will maintain a studied reserve. Let the plain facts speak. I claim the utmost attention to them, for their importance is immense. The Higher Critics admit that "the Divine authority and revelation of the Old Testament" was expressly taught by the Lord Jesus Christ. But to avoid the consequences of this admission, they represent that in this matter the Lord was the dupe of "a current Jewish notion," or in other words, of an ignorant error. And this, remember, is not the position or language of the extreme section represented by Professor Cheyne, but of the "cautious" and "conservative" English critics of Professor Driver's school.

To raise the question, as some do, whether the Lord was versed in higher mathematics or the discoveries of modern science, would be a mere quibble were it not for its profanity. And the objection that in childhood He must have been subject to the limitations of childhood is wholly irrelevant. For it is with the Christ of the Ministry that we have to do. And the question does not relate to limitations upon knowledge in matters as to which He was silent, but to ignorance leading to teaching which the critics allege to be false and mischievous, on subjects of vital moment to His disciples and to the Church for all time. But even this is not all. When He appeared to His disciples after His resurrection, not only did He not revise the teaching of the days of His humiliation, but He repeated it with increased definiteness. [1]

1] The "Jesus" of Matthew Arnold, the agnostic, is "manifestly above the heads of his reporters" (Lit. and Dogma, Pref. 1888); the "Jesus" of these writers who claim to be Christians, is manifestly on a level with them.

Counsel in a lawsuit has sometimes to advise that unless some adverse witness can be discredited, the case must collapse. In this Higher Criticism campaign, the witness who must be discredited is our Divine Lord. No straining of the doctrine of the Kenosis will cover this: it brings us within sight of the great Anti-christian apostasy of the latter days. [1]

> 1] There lies before me as I write, the current number of a weekly religious paper which has done yeoman's service in the Higher Criticism crusade. It contains a fierce attack upon Prof. Cheyne and the third volume of his Encyclopedia. I turn the page to find a notice of an able and valuable little book of the Rev. David M'Intyre, of Glasgow, entitled *The Divine Authority of the Scriptures of the Old Testament*; and here I read, "All this citation of passages is useless, unless it first be made good that our Lord's knowledge of critical questions was different from that of his contemporaries." This suggests Dr. Pusey's words, "I know not whether the open blasphemy of the eighteenth century is more offensive than the cold-blooded patronizing ways of the nineteenth." Can anything well go further than this—that in His apprehension of the very Scriptures which testified of Himself, our Lord was less intelligent than the editor and staff of this newspaper! I would wish to believe that the words were written hurriedly and thoughtlessly.

As we proceed, then, let us keep these two facts clearly in view. First, that the Lord Jesus Christ regarded the Old Testament as Divinely inspired in the very sense in which all these critics repudiate inspiration; and secondly, that the only escape from that conclusion is to disparage either His teaching or the record of it. And this is to destroy Christianity altogether.

Even Professor Cheyne and his school accept the personality of "the historic Jesus." He was they tell us, "undoubtedly a devout Jew;" and as the traditional teaching of this traditional Jesus is superior to that of Mahomet or Gautama, "the Christian religion" would no doubt survive the collapse of Christianity. But that is not what concerns us here. The Christian is not the votary of the best of all human religions. He is the recipient of a Divine revelation which has brought Him the knowledge of salvation in a personal Savior, and has made him the redeemed disciple of a personal Lord and Master. We are followers, not of the historic Jesus of the critics— the dead Buddha of nineteen centuries ago—but of the Lord Jesus Christ, the

Only-begotten Son of God, who "died for our sins according to the Scriptures." [1]

1] 1 Cor. 15:3.

Now any clear thinker can see that if, in the words I have just quoted, "the Scriptures" mean mere human records, this whole system rests upon a foundation of sand. The death of " the historic Jesus" is a fact so well accredited that no transcendental proof of it is needed. But that "Christ died for our sins" is a fact which nothing but a Divine revelation could possibly accredit. Therefore it is that those who give up inspiration generally end in giving up the atonement.

But Christ "rose again the third day, according to the Scriptures." What Scriptures? The reference is to the Old Testament, of course. But where does the Old Testament tell us that Christ would die for our sins and rise again the third day? Here comes in the force of Dean Alford's words: "The whole Scriptures are a testimony to Him; the whole history of the chosen people, with its types, its law, and its prophecies."

But just as the unbelieving Jews were entirely taken up with the humanity of the Lord Jesus Christ, and He was nothing to them but "the carpenter's son," so these critics are engrossed with the human side of Scripture. Its deep spiritual significance they ignore. They study the tapestry upon the wrong side, and write ponderous tomes replete with important and useful information of every kind about the materials used in the making of it, and the men who wove it, and the marvelous way it was put together at different periods and how it has been preserved to our own day. But its chief defect —natural enough, having regard to its history—is the utter want of design or pattern of any kind. We, however, who look at the fabric upon the upper side are filled with admiration at its symmetry and beauty. And as we think of the Master mind that planned it, and mark the way in which every detail of His plan has been realized, all that those who are busy plodding at the other side of it can tell us serves only to deepen our wonder and to increase our delight.

Chapter 7

We have seen that our belief in God tends to a belief in the existence of a written revelation. And having reached this point it would be idle pedantry to discuss the rival claims of the Bible and of other books. Moreover, I am writing for Christians, and with the Christian the only question open is— How, and to what extent, is the Bible inspired? Now it is admitted that the Lord Jesus Christ has taught us to reverence the Hebrew Scriptures as inspired in the strictest sense. And we have seen that if part at least of the New Testament be not inspired in that same sense, there is no rational basis for believing any of the transcendental truths of Christianity.

What concerns us, then, is the method of the inspiration. And the first question which arises may be popularly stated thus, Whether did God inspire the Scriptures, or the men who wrote them? Now I am not going to enter on this well-worn controversy. Were I to restate the question and ask, Are the Scriptures inspired writings? or Are they the writings of inspired men? it would need a lengthy chapter to explain the point at issue. I take note of the fact, first, that the Bible itself advances no theory of inspiration; and secondly, that none was ever formulated until modern times. And further, I would urge that between these rival theories there is no such antithesis as the controversy supposes.

True it is that "Saul among the prophets" became a proverb; and a dumb ass was once inspired to rebuke a prophet. But not even the Higher Critics have suggested that either Balaam's Ass or the Son of Kish made any contribution to the written revelation. If by inspired men be meant men filled with the Spirit, and specially guided by the Spirit, then we may assert with confidence that the Biblical writers were inspired men.

Which of course will call out the taunt, Was David one of your "inspired men"? That sneer shall be answered in the words of a rugged, honest-hearted man of the world: —

> "David, the Hebrew king, had fallen into sins enough; blackest crimes; there was no want of sins. And therefore the unbelievers sneer and ask, Is this your man according to God's heart? The sneer, I must say, seems to me but a shallow one. What are faults, what are the outward details of a life, if the inner secret of it, the remorse, temptations, true often-baffled, never-ended struggle of it, be forgotten? 'It is not in man that walketh to direct his steps.' Of all acts, is not, for a man, repentance the most divine? The deadliest sin, I say, were that same supercilious consciousness of no sin;—that is death; the heart so conscious is divorced from sincerity, humility and fact; is dead: it is 'pure' as dead dry sand is pure. David's life and history, as written for us in those Psalms of his, I consider to be the truest emblem ever given of a man's moral progress and warfare here below. All earnest souls will ever discern in it the faithful struggle of an earnest human soul towards what is good and best. Struggle often baffled, sore baffled, down as into entire wreck ; yet a struggle never ended; ever, with tears, repentance, true unconquerable purpose, begun anew." (Thomas Carlyle, *Heroes*, Sect. II.)

A passing word about the "blackest crimes." I am no apologist of evil. But the matter of Uriah's wife I leave to each man to settle with his own conscience, asking him only not to forget the facts. Most men cater for the sin which brings them down; but the temptation which led to David's fall was not of his seeking. By accident it was that Bathsheba crossed his path. Nor did he even know that she was married. And when he had brought the woman into peril, he tried to save her by recalling her husband to Jerusalem. But in this he was foiled by Uriah's keenness as a soldier. He was bent on "returning to the front"; and drunk or sober he could not be turned from his purpose. The wretched king was thus confronted by the fact that the death of the man he had wronged was the only possible way to save the woman he had tempted. The horrible doom of the unfaithful wife awaited her. And in desperation he framed the guilty plot. It is a terrible instance of what men have so often proved, that one sin always leads to another, and immorality often leads to crime. The only unique element in David's case was the depth and permanency of his repentance. Here is the Divine summary of his life story: "Save only in the matter of Uriah the Hittite, David did right in the eyes of the Lord, and turned not aside from anything that He commanded him all the days of his life." [1] No wonder that he was "a man after God's heart!" [2]

>1] 1 Kings 15:5.

>2] See Professor Margoliouth's striking passage on this subject in his *Defence of the Biblical Revelation*, pp. 209, 210.

Yes, it was men like David that God used to write the Bible. And the fifty-first Psalm betokens more fitness for the part than the smug pharisaic and self-confidence of all the critics of Christendom.

There is no doubt that the writers were inspired men. And those whose lives are unfolded to us were severely trained in the school of God. They knew the meaning of the crucible and the refiner's fire. As the apostles proved in later times, they were made a spectacle to angels and to men. Visions of unutterable glory, like those vouchsafed to Isaiah and Ezekiel, alternated with sufferings that tore their very heartstrings. And here it may be said in passing, that no one can even understand the Scriptures who is entirely a stranger to experiences like those of the men who wrote them. We can beat back attacks by exposing ignorance and folly and error, and turning the weapons of assailants against themselves. But "the natural man receiveth not the things of the Spirit of God, for they are foolishness unto him; neither can he know them, because they are spiritually discerned." [1] And the tenor of a spiritual life is the path of discipleship, and discipleship means being a partaker of the sufferings of Him who was called "the Man of Sorrows," as well as a sharer of the joy that is unspeakable and of the peace that passes understanding.

>1] 1 Cor. 2:14.

But some will say, "All this is unreservedly conceded: the men who wrote the Scriptures were inspired, and inspired to write them; and therefore their writings are inspired. But though the thoughts were divinely given them, the words in which they expressed them were their own. Our difficulty springs from the dogma of verbal inspiration."

Chapter 7

Now first, let us face the facts; and they are facts some of which a certain phase of dull "orthodoxy" blindly ignores. A critical examination of the text will satisfy us that, for example, the prophecies of Isaiah were written in Isaiah's language, and those of Jeremiah in Jeremiah's language, and so on. The inference drawn from this is that, even assuming that God suggested the ideas, each writer must have been left free to express them in his own words; and therefore that inspiration is no guarantee of accuracy Whether this be so or not, must be decided on other grounds. To base it on the ground stated involves the fallacy of supposing that God has a language of His own, and therefore that human words cannot have a Divine authority.

A more egregious fallacy there could not be. The connection between language and thought is one of the most interesting problems of metaphysics. But words are merely sounds; and in one sense the relation between a word and the idea it represents to a trained mind is as arbitrary as that which a note on the piano bears to the musical sound produced by striking it. A trained mind, I say, because if the idea be not there, the sound will not call it up.

But, it will be objected, words have a history, and therefore they are not mere arbitrarily chosen sounds. True, but this only adds force to my argument. Some new idea arises in the mind, or some new object is presented to it. The existing vocabulary contains no word to represent it, and a new one is framed to supply the want.

To those, therefore, who frame the word, it seems to carry its own meaning; but this is due solely to its connection with the mental processes which led to its birth. To others it is but a sound. For example, the fraudulent way in which "escheats" were formerly seized by the Crown led to the creation of the word "cheat"; but there is not one person in ten thousand who now thinks of its origin, and to such it is a mere sound which they have learned to connect with a particular idea.

If a man has not the conception which we associate with the word "eternal," the word, even though it were emblazoned across the sky, could not evoke it. And shouting *olam* or *aionios* into his ear would be mere noise to him. "Words are the counters of wise men, the money of fools." They represent ideas, but they have no intrinsic value. And, as I have said, their relation to the ideas they represent is arbitrary. Write pain on a piece of paper, and show it on Dover pier:

you will be referred to a doctor. Cross the Channel and exhibit it at Calais: you will be directed to the refreshment-room. [1]

> 1] Someone may object that the sound would be different. Very well. At Calais, call out the French word for lady, and they may imagine you have lost a travelling companion : at Dover they would certainly think you most profane.

The argument is that as Isaiah, for example, wrote in his own language, his writings cannot be called "the Word of God." Will the critics tell us in what language other than his own the prophet could have written? If a man makes a communication to another, he conveys it either in his own language, or in that of the recipient But as God has no language of His own, He speaks to men in theirs. Would the Bible be more Divine if it were written in some celestial *Volapuk* [an artificial language created in 1879], with a superadded miracle, unparalleled in the whole range of recorded miracles, to make men understand it? A nice sort of Bible that would be!

Of course, God could have made all the prophets use the same words and idioms as the earliest of them. But what would have been gained by this? Some people would persuade us that the English race now holds the place once held by Israel. If this were so, and God were to give us a special revelation today, it would not be in ancient Hebrew, but in modern English. Even supposing, for example, that Yahweh is the correct orthography of the great covenant name, we may be quite sure that Jehovah is the name by which God would call Himself in addressing us —that name which is enshrined in the religious thought and worship of all the English-speaking races of the world. For Yahweh would be mere jargon save to the Hebraist; and it is very doubtful whether the Hebraist's knowledge of the etymology of the term would not mislead him as to its significance.

Take these words, for instance: "The Lord Jehovah is my strength and my song; He also is become my salvation." [1] Now to the believer, as such, the question of the spelling or the etymology of the name is of no more importance than that of the type in which it is printed. The only practical question is whether he has the conception which the name is intended to call up. The name was in use from primeval times: it was the great covenant name of God. But it was not till He identified Himself with an earthly people that men could know what it really meant to have a Jehovah God. [2]

>1] Isa. 12:2.
>
>2] This is the meaning of Exod. 6:3 (see Appendix, Note I). I venture to suggest that the use of Yahweh, or Yahveh, savours of pedantry. It is justified on two grounds; 1st, traditional authority (for the contempt which the critics feel for "traditional beliefs" does not apply if the tradition be Rabbinical); and 2ndly, that it carries its own meaning. To which plea I answer that its etymological meaning is not its meaning as used in Scripture. It is not an English word, and its use is therefore precisely the same kind of pedantry as, e.g., using Firenze instead of Florence.
>
>The vowels of our magnificent word Jehovah are accounted for thus: The old Hebrew MSS. had no vowels, but when the name occurred, the Jews suppressed it from feelings of reverence, and read Adonai instead; and the vowels of this name were inserted under the line to remind the reader of the keri, or word to be read. As a matter of fact, the name was uttered daily in the blessing of the priests (*Diet. Christ. Ant.*, vol. 1, p. 198); and the spelling of the many names with which it is incorporated (such as *Je*hoida, *Jeho*shaphat, etc.) would indicate that Jehovah may be correct. Yahveh is a mere guess which may be right or may be wrong.

Some men, no doubt, would be better satisfied with the Bible if all the prophets had written in exactly the same dialect and style; and better still if they had written in Pauline Greek or modern English. That would have been a miracle indeed, and really worth notice! Of course, God might have inspired the Scriptures in this way. Yes, and the Lord might have fed the multitudes without using up the disciples' little store of loaves and fishes. But this is not His way. Divine power summoned Lazarus from the grave, but it was left to human hands to loose him from the grave-clothes. Divine power called Jairus's daughter back to life, but her parents were commanded to give her food. [1] It appears to be a principle with God never to put forth Divine power save in so far as human means are inadequate or unavailable. And anyone who grasps this principle holds a clue to the solution of many a difficulty in this matter of inspiration. It is a principle which mars the dramatic effect of most of the miracles, the miracle of inspiration not excepted; but dramatic effect is not studied in Divine miracles at all.

1] Luke 8:55.

In this aspect of it, then, the verbal inspiration difficulty is unworthy of notice. The only question of any practical importance is whether, as the New Testament so plainly teaches, God spoke "through" (or "in") the writers of the Old. But just as the morbidly inquisitive brain of a certain sort of child insists on seeing inside a watch, when sober common sense asks only whether it can be trusted to tell the time; so while "the common sense of faith" is content to know that God inspired the Bible, there are minds that demand to know all the mysteries of the problem of inspiration. And some people think they have solved these mysteries, just as there are men who fancy they have mastered the infinite wonders of Nature. But wiser heads distinguish between the facts, whether of revelation or of nature, and the theories which men offer in explanation of them. We do well to accept with intelligent and unfaltering confidence the fact of inspiration so clearly taught by our Divine Lord; but we do well also to view with great distrust all human theories relating to it.

"But," someone will here interrupt, "anybody can see the difference between a man's recording matters within his own knowledge, and matters or truths of which he could know nothing except by direct revelation." Yes, anybody can see it. And after he has seen it, what then? Does the interrupter mean, for example, that the prophet is to be believed implicitly when he declares that "the ransomed of the Lord shall return, and come to Zion with songs, and everlasting joy upon their heads" [1]; but that he is not to be trusted when in the next sentence he records that "In the fourteenth year of king Hezekiah, Sennacherib king of Assyria came up against all the defended cities of Judah and took them." [2] And if he does not mean this, what sense is there in the interruption? Anyone but a Higher Critic would test a chain at the weakest link, and not at the strongest. He would say, "If you can satisfy me that God made the prophet write those words about future blessing for Zion, I shall have no doubt about the Sennacherib invasion." The problem has difficulties for those who want to frame theories of inspiration; but the Christian who merely wants to be assured that the truth of Scripture is Divinely guaranteed, brushes the difficulties aside.

1] Isa. 35:10.

2] Ibid. 36:1.

"But," the objector says again, "the manner in which the Old Testament is quoted in the New — loosely quoted sometimes from the notoriously loose Septuagint translation — explodes all your theories of verbal inspiration." Well, so much the worse for the theories. But will the objector tell us in what way this affects the fact of inspiration. The Bible was not written for the wise of this world; still less for fools. To understand it aright we need both spiritual intelligence and common sense. The latter quality will help us here. Anyone who possesses it can see that in the historical narrative of Isaiah 36-39, for example, the sense is everything, and the choice of words is a matter of comparative indifference. Whereas in chapters 35 and 40 absolute verbal accuracy may possibly be essential. And so we find sometimes a quotation so loosely given that care is needed to trace it to its source, while in other cases emphasis is laid upon the very tense of a verb or the number of a noun. It is not that in the one case the statement is less true than in the other, but that less importance, or possibly none, attaches to the particular words used to express it.

Instances of this are familiar to every Bible student. Here, for example, is one of them. Of those who denied the resurrection, the Lord demanded, "Have ye not read that which was spoken unto you by God, saying, I am the God of Abraham, and the God of Isaac, and the God of Jacob? God is not the God of the dead, but of the living." [1] Now here the whole force of the argument depends on the tense of the verb. To say that the language of Exodus means merely that God was the God of the patriarchs, would be quite in keeping with the loose way the Bible is treated by the critics. But the word is not I was the God of Abraham, but "I Am the God of Abraham"; and therefore Abraham is still an existing person, a person in being. And as a clue to the use of Scripture, it is noteworthy that these words were spoken "by God," and spoken to those whom the Lord was then addressing.

1] Matt. 22:31, 32.

Take another instance still more striking. "Is it not written in your law, 'I said, Ye are gods'? If He called them gods to whom the word of God came (and the Scripture cannot be broken), say ye, etc." Now here Psa. 82 is ascribed to God, and not to the Psalmist; it is declared to be Scripture which cannot be broken; and it is appealed to as making "an end of controversy." And as in the other case, the force of the argument depends on the absolute accuracy of the words. [1]

> 1] John 10:34, 35. The critics meet all this by representing the Lord as an ignorant person and the Evangelists as being untrustworthy. See Chapters 6 and 19.

We see, then, how and why a Divine revelation must be made in the language of those to whom it comes. And upon their fitness and capacity to receive it depend any limits and failure of the revelation. For words are merely like paper securities for money. Intrinsically valueless, their worth depends on the gold they represent. If the gold be wanting, the paper is only paper and nothing more. If the thoughts the words represent are absent, the words are only empty sounds. Therefore it is that inspired men are needed to be the channels of a revelation, and spiritual men alone can understand it aright.

"Behold, God is my salvation; I will trust and not be afraid: for the Lord Jehovah is my strength and my song; He also is become my salvation." We are dependent on Hebrew scholars to give us these English words: we are absolutely dependent on the Spirit of God to enable us to understand them. True exegesis consists in "interpreting spiritual things to spiritual men." [1] And therefore Hebrew scholars as such cannot help us here; for they can only explain natural things to natural men.

> 1] 1 Cor. 2:13, R.V. margin.

Chapter 8

When Xerxes issued his great proclamation in favor of the Jews, it was sent, we are told, to each of the hundred and twenty-seven provinces of the Empire, from India to Ethiopia, "and unto every people after their language." [1] Could any of the nations have pleaded a wrong or a disability because the royal commands reached them only in their own dialect or tongue? Was this not altogether an advantage and a benefit? We may be sure that the great king would have made short work of such a grievance, and of those who urged it. He would have judged, and rightly judged, that the objection was merely an excuse for disaffection or disobedience.

1] Esther 8.

And yet one of the popular objections urged against "verbal inspiration" as a practical truth is that ordinary Christians being ignorant of the language in which the revelation was given are entirely dependent on translations. But this is only another phase of the very difficulty discussed in the preceding chapter. It is based upon the fallacy of supposing that words have any intrinsic or essential meaning. As we have seen, the ablest Hebraist in Christendom has not necessarily any better knowledge of the Old Testament revelation than the humblest Christian who enjoys the benefit of his learned labors. And if he be not spiritually enlightened, it may be confidently assumed that the humble Christian will have the advantage. The pundit indeed can trace words to their roots, but this sort of inquiry, important and interesting though it be to the philologist, may for practical purposes prove misleading. The meaning of a word depends, not upon its origin, but upon its use; and its use may vary at different periods of a language's development. For example, one whom we call an uncultured peasant our forefathers would have described as a "lewd villain"; and a clever youth they would have called a "crafty knave."

Every ancient language has a history; but while the history of modern English, and, to a certain extent, of New Testament Greek, is open to our view, the steps by which the language of Moses and the prophets had reached the stage of what we call sacred Hebrew, are unknown. One thing is certain, namely, that the language of the Old Testament, like that of the New, was an adaptation to high and sacred uses of words which had been current in pagan communities. And this being so, it might be plausibly contended that our own language, having been formed and molded upon Christian thought, is a fitter vehicle for the communication of Divine truth even than the Hebrew of the prophets or the Greek of the apostles and evangelists. Words are but counters; and counters which were rescued from base or vulgar uses may not be so fit to stand for the gold of revealed truth as ours which never have been thus prostituted.

Take an illustration. The English peasant who hears of eternal life through faith in Christ may grasp fully and at once the truth those words convey; while the Jewish peasant was much in the position of an Englishman with some newfangled translation which tells him of "age-enduring life through faith in the Anointed One."

As a matter of fact the heresies of the eschatological controversy largely depend on the undoubted fact that neither ancient Hebrew nor classical Greek had any term equivalent to our English word "Eternal." The Pagan mind had no such conception. Their highest thought was of prolonged existence in time, whereas eternal life in Christ is outside the sphere of time both in its origin and in its continuance.

Or take a different sort of case. If the word "priest" suggests a false conception to a man's mind, the study of its Hebrew or Greek equivalent will in no way correct the error. During a summer holiday in the West of Ireland I once had opportunities of addressing Roman Catholics, and I conceived the plan of weaning them from the errors of their creed by speaking of the priesthood of Christ. But I found that while my words were Scriptural and right, the meaning they conveyed to my hearers was wholly false and wrong. They understood me to mean that what Roman Catholic priests were and did, Christ was and did.

And this experience gave me the clue to the meaning of the closing verses of the fifth chapter of Hebrews. The Hebrew Christians, in ignorance, as the writer says, of the rudiments even of revealed religion, assumed that there was a necessary connection between the office of a priest and the offering of sacrifices for sins; [1] and therefore the doctrine of the priesthood of Christ operated in their case to undermine one of the great truths of the Epistle, that "there is no more offering for sin." [2]

> 1] Ignorance which the most elementary knowledge of Scripture ought to have removed; for there were sacrifices long before there were priests. The words of Heb. 5:12 (R.V.) are, "Ye have need that one teach you again which be the rudiments of the first principles of the oracles of God." The words of 6:1 are, "the first principles of Christ." The one refers to revealed religion generally, the other to the special revelation of Judaism.
>
> 2] At Professor Sanday's *Oxford Conference* on this subject, the Rev. Mr. Puller, of the "Cowley Fathers," was the only member who seemed to grasp the elementary truth that the work of priesthood began after the sacrifice had been killed, and that the priesthood of Christ dates from His ascension. "On earth He could not be a priest at all" (Heb. 8:4, R.V.).
>
> The R.V. of Heb. 5:1 makes havoc of the truth. It tells us that every high priest is taken from among men, and is appointed to offer sacrifices for sins. The teaching of the verse is correctly given in A.V., that every high-priest-taken-from-among-men (i.e., every Aaronic priest) is appointed for that purpose. But our High Priest is "the Son of God" (4:14), and His priesthood is based upon the Sacrifice which has for ever put away sin, so that now "there is no more offering for sin" (10:18).

All objections to verbal inspiration which are based on the phenomena of language may be ruled out, for they rest on no substantial foundation. That a revelation could be made only in human language is a necessity from the limitations of human thought; and how there can be language without words —how there can be inspiration other than verbal inspiration —is a metaphysical problem which I confess I am not clever enough to be able to solve. [1] And the question whether a revelation gains or loses by being translated from one language into another depends on whether the language into which it is rendered is better or worse fitted to clothe and express the thoughts contained in it.

> 1] Of course a revelation may be by way of visions, as in the Apocalypse; but this only puts the question one step back.

The objections which some writers urge against verbal inspiration are analogous to those which other writers urge against belief in a personal God who thinks and loves. They call this "anthropomorphism." But let no one be scared at being called by such a hard name. They who use it —very superior persons they are —are like silly children who ape full-grown people. When the silly children discover their folly by some disaster, they can be whipped and put to bed; but the philosophers may not discover theirs until it be too late for repentance. We do not assume that God really has ears and nostrils and hands and feet, any more than that He has a language of His own. But the wisest and best of us are like children —very young and very foolish children, —and as He pities us as a father pities his children, He speaks to us about Himself in a way we can understand. Let no one, then, be cajoled or browbeaten into the mingled pedantry and silliness and sin of thinking we are wiser than He is, or that we can do without verbal inspiration and the God of the Bible.

But an objection of another kind remains. The original records of the Divine revelation have been lost, and vast periods of time separate us from them. For example, some five and thirty centuries have passed since Moses wrote, and yet the oldest Hebrew record we possess of his writings was probably written after the time of Alfred the Great of England. We deem it a disadvantage to have access only to a copy of an important document, but here it is a case of repeated copying during thousands of years, and in circumstances of which we know but little.

Now this objection is a real one, and it must be owned that at first sight it seems extremely formidable. But its practical importance grows less and less the more closely we examine it.

In the first place, the special importance to us of the Hebrew Scriptures depends on their relation to Christianity; and as the Jew was the custodian of them, it is certain that if they have been willfully tampered with, the change has not been made in the interests of Christian truth. But in the second place, the extreme reverence with

Chapter 8

which the Jews regarded their Scriptures affords a powerful guarantee against any deliberate corruption of the text. It may be taken as certain that any errors which have crept in are errors accidentally made in copying the manuscripts. And when estimating the number and, what is of more importance, the character of such errors, the Jewish reverence for the text claims very special consideration. For it insured such care in copying as to make any blunder of a really serious kind improbable in the extreme.

We know, for example, that in the days of the Massoretes, to whom we practically owe our text of the Old Testament, not only the words, but the very letters, contained in the sacred books were counted. And we know also that even when words were believed to have been erroneously inserted or omitted, the scribes never dared to make a correction save by a marginal note. And there is no reason to doubt that these practices were based on the habits and traditions of earlier days.

Hostile critics have sometimes sought to score a point by appealing to the Samaritan Pentateuch and the Septuagint version. But not even a hostile critic would deny that if the Massoretic text were revised in the light of those authorities, the result would be prejudicial to accuracy; and, further, that even if the revision were drastic and reckless, it would not affect a single question of morals or a single point of Christian truth or doctrine. And this being so, the whole question, so far as the Old Testament is concerned, is one of purely academic interest.

And a kindred remark applies equally in regard to the New Testament. A fact which is all the more striking and important because the materials for hostile criticism here are vastly greater than in the case of the Old Testament. All our leading commentators have grappled with the question. As it has been well said,

> "All of them face that formidable phantom of textual criticism, with its 120,000 various readings in the New Testament alone, and will enable us to march up to it, and discover that it is empty air; that still we may say with the boldest and acutest of English critics, Bentley, 'choose (out of the whole MSS.) as awkwardly as you will, choose the worst by design out of the whole lump of readings, and not one article of faith or moral precept is either perverted or lost in them. Put them into the hands of a knave or a fool, and even with the most sinister and

absurd choice, he shall not extinguish the light of any one chapter, or so disguise Christianity but that every feature of it will still be the same.'"

These words have since received most striking confirmation. In the Revised Version of the New Testament textual criticism has done its worst . It is inconceivable that it will ever again be allowed to run riot as in the work of the Revisers of 1881. When that version appeared, Bishop Wordsworth of Lincoln raised the question "whether the Church of England, — which in her Synod, so far as this Province is concerned, sanctioned a Revision of her Authorized Version under the express condition, which she most wisely imposed, that no changes should be made in it except what were absolutely necessary, —could consistently accept a version in which 36,000 changes have been made; not a fiftieth of which can be shown to be needed, or even desirable."

But what concerns us here is not the changes in the translation, but the far more serious matter of the changes in the text. The question at issue between the majority of the Revisers, who followed Doctors Hort and Westcott, and the very able and weighty minority led by Dr. Scrivener, the most capable and eminent "textual critic" of the whole company, was one with which every lawyer is familiar, but of which the Revisers may have had no experience, and with which they were not competent to deal.

We have a far greater number of MSS. of the New Testament than of the heathen classics; but, strange to say, with four exceptions, none of these are older than the sixth century of our era. But we possess "versions" (or translations) which are older than any known MSS.; and the writings of the early Fathers abound in quotations from the New Testament. [1] We are thus enabled indirectly to reach MSS. much older than the oldest that have survived. And as the Fathers were scattered over the Christendom of their time, their acquaintance with the text was derived, of course, from very many independent sources. And when their quotations agree with one another, and also with the "versions," as well as with our later MSS., many of which must have been copied from MSS. more ancient than any which have survived, this agreement will satisfy any one who is versed in the rudiments of the science of evidence.

> 1] It has been said that if the Gospels were lost the text could be regained, with trifling gaps, from the writings of

the AnteNicene Fathers. (Dr. Sinker's Higher Criticism, p. 177.)

But while the lawyer understands the value of indirect evidence, the layman is always inclined to disparage it in favor of the direct. Witnesses of credit and repute testify that they saw the accused commit the crime with which he is charged. What more can anyone want? The average juryman is ready at once to convict; and he cannot imagine why the judge should allow further time to be spent upon the case. But the judge knows well that evidence of this kind is apt to err, and needs to be tested with the utmost care. [1] Now the old MSS. are the witnesses of credit and repute, and the Revisers played the part of the average juryman; and there being unfortunately no one to check them, they convicted the Authorized Version of inaccuracy in numberless instances. But, in the opinion of the greatest critical authority among the Revisers, whose protests were unavailing to prevent this deplorable mutilation of the sacred text, the system on which these changes were made "is entirely destitute of historical foundation." [2]

> 1] Of course, if the accused is seized at the time, the evidence of eye-witnesses is conclusive. The conflict between direct and indirect evidence arises where the accused is arrested after an interval, and his identity becomes the salient question in the case.
>
> 2] Dr. Scrivener, Plain Introduction, etc.

If the Revisers had kept to the terms of their commission, and been content with the correction of "manifest errors," a very few sessions would have sufficed to produce a text which might have commanded universal acceptance. But it is certain that errors were not manifest when many of the greatest of contemporary critics and scholars could not regard them as errors at all — men like the minority upon their own company, men like the eminent prelate I have quoted, and the learned editor of The Speaker's Commentary. And as several of the Revisers themselves have explained in detail the principles on which the revision of the text was conducted, and those principles are found to be unsound when judged by the science of evidence, our confidence in the result of their labors is destroyed.

The "argument" of the present volume demands a reference to

this question, but a fuller discussion of it would be out of place. I will therefore dismiss it by citing a single illustrative instance of reckless and erroneous alteration of the text. And instances of the kind abound, especially in the Gospels.

The instance I select is "the Herald Angels' song," and I choose it not only as being thoroughly typical of the methods of the Revisers, but also because of its importance and the interest attaching to it. "Glory to God in the highest, and on earth peace, good will toward men": [1] for these words, which hold such a place in the memory and heart of every English-speaking Christian, the miserable substitute offered us is, "Glory to God in the highest, and on earth peace among men in whom He is well pleased." This one piece of mutilation might suffice to discredit the work of the Revisers.

> 1] Luke 2:14.

Two questions are here involved, the altered text, and the translation of that text. The English of the Revisers, says one of the most eminent of their own number, "can be arrived at only through some process which would make any phrase bear almost any meaning the translator might like to put upon it." [1] "'Men in whom He is well pleased,'" says the editor of *The Speaker's Commentary*, "seems to me impossible as a translation of ἄνθρωποι εὐζοκίας."

> 1] Dr. Scrivener's Introduction (Ed. Miller), vol. 2, p. 347.

I do not know whether those Greek words have any meaning, but if they have they must designate men of a certain quality or character." [1] Then as regards the text, the whole difference is the addition of the letter *s* to the word *eudokia*; and the manuscript authority for this addition is the reading of four ancient Greek MSS., [2] every other known copy of the Gospels being against it.

> 1] *R.V. of the First Three Gospels*, p. 30. Canon Cook adds, "What is meant by the marginal rendering 'men of good pleasure' I am utterly at a loss to conjecture."
>
> 2] Canon Cook enumerates them as the Sinaitic, and A, B, and D, and he adds that the text of the first and third of these "was noted as incorrect by a critical scholar at the time when the manuscript was written" (Ibid., pp. 27, 28).

Now this is precisely the sort of question in respect of which anyone who has practical acquaintance with the science of evidence would appeal to Patristic authority, and that appeal would dispose of the whole matter; for the testimony of the Greek Fathers in favor of the familiar reading is overwhelming. [1]

> 1] In *The Revision Revised* (pp. 42-44), Dean Burgon gives the list of Fathers from the second to the sixth century, indicating that the words as known to us, i.e., as given in our A.V., were quoted by them fifty-eight times. Speaking generally, the Greek authorities are on the side of the A.V.; while the R.V. can appeal to the Latin versions. This is remarkable, but the explanation of it is simple. Some ancient MS. upon which the first Latin version was based, evidently omitted the preposition from the sentence, and as this destroyed its meaning the s was added to *eudokia* to make the words intelligible.

"On earth peace, good will toward men" — the Christian may still rejoice in these hallowed and most precious words. And he may assume with confidence that here, as in so many other instances, the Revisers' changes in the text are new errors, and not the correction of old errors. And yet the fact remains —indeed it is universally acknowledged —that even a revision conducted so unwisely and on a system so opposed to all the principles and rules of evidence, has not destroyed a single truth of Christianity or left a single point of Christian doctrine or practice in jeopardy. The skeptical taunt that textual criticism undermines the truth of Inspiration is forever silenced by the Revised Version of the New Testament. [1]

> 1] See App. Note II.

Chapter 9

Some there are who will have read the preceding chapters with sympathy, who yet will feel that their own special difficulties remain unnoticed. They love the Bible, and are assured that it is in the main Divine, but there is much in the Old Testament which unduly tries their faith. "The creation story of Genesis," they would say, "is discredited by science. The Book of Jonah is incredible. The Book of Daniel can no longer be defended. The history of Israel is marked by moral difficulties which cannot be explained away. And no one can now defend the correctness of Old Testament chronology.

"Nor are these difficulties confined to the Old Testament. Whatever theoretical defense may be made for the inspiration of the Gospels, the fact remains that they are marked by errors which prove that, if they be inspired, inspiration affords no guarantee of truth."

With these several questions I will now proceed to deal. [1] And first as to "the proem to Genesis." If I were beginning an octavo volume, I should seek to recapitulate the controversy on this subject, and to define the stage it has at present reached. I should mark the various positions which have been successively occupied or abandoned by the disputants, as one or another of the fluctuating theories of science has gained prominence, or newly found fossils have added to "the testimony of the rocks." But I will content myself with recalling the main incidents of the discussion between Mr. Gladstone and Professor Huxley some years ago in the pages of the *Nineteenth Century*. [2]

> 1] This chapter is based in part upon Chapter VIII. of the author's Doubter's Doubts about Science and Religion—a book long out of print.
>
> 2] The articles in question appeared in the later months of 1885, and January and February, 1886.

Chapter 9

In *The Dawn of Creation and Worship* Mr. Gladstone sought to show that the order of creation as recorded in Genesis has been "so affirmed in our time by natural science that it may be taken as a demonstrated conclusion and established fact." He averred that science was perfectly in accord with Moses in recognizing that life appeared upon our globe in the order of, first, the water population; second, the air population; and, third, the land population. To which Mr. Huxley replied as follows: —

> "It is agreed on all hands that terrestrial lizards and other reptiles allied to lizards occur in the Permian strata. It is further agreed that the Triassic strata were deposited after these. Moreover, it is well known that, even if certain footprints are to be taken as unquestionable evidence of the existence of birds, they are not known to occur in rocks earlier than the Trias, while indubitable remains of birds are to be met with only much later. Hence it follows that natural science does not 'affirm' the statement that birds were made on the fifth day, and 'everything that creepeth on the ground' on the sixth, on which Mr. Gladstone rests his order; for, as is shown by Leviticus, the 'Mosaic writer' includes lizards among his 'creeping things.'"

The following is the quotation from Leviticus which Mr. Huxley "commended to Mr. Gladstone's serious attention":— "And these are they which are unclean unto you among the creeping things that creep upon the earth; the weasel, and the mouse, and the great lizard after its kind, and the gecko, and the land-crocodile, and the lizard, and the sand-lizard, and the chameleon. These are they which are unclean unto you among all that creep" (chap. 11:29-31, R.V.). And he added, "The merest Sunday-school exegesis, therefore, suffices to prove that when the Mosaic writer in Gen. 1:24 speaks of creeping things, he means to include lizards among them."

A charming specimen this certainly is of "the merest Sunday-school exegesis." The argument which so completely satisfied its author, and silenced his opponent, is nothing but an *ad captandum* appeal to the chance rendering of our English Bible. For the word translated "creeping thing" in Leviticus 11 has no affinity with the word so rendered in Genesis 1:24, whereas it is the identical word which our translators have rendered "moving creature" in the twentieth verse, which records the first appearance of animal life. [1]

> 1] The word in verses 24 and 26, relating to the life of the sixth day, is *remes*; but in verse 20, relating to the fifth day, it is *sheretz*, which occurs ten times in Lev. 11.

Mr. Huxley's answer was, therefore, an overwhelming refutation of his own position. Science proclaims the seniority of land reptiles in the genesis of life on earth, and the despised Book of Genesis records that "creeping things," which, as Mr. Huxley insists, must include land reptiles, were the first "moving creatures" which the Creator's fiat called into existence.

Some may think that if Mr. Huxley were still with us he could make short work of this. But the plea will not avail. In the *Times* correspondence of ten years ago on *The Bible and Modern Criticism*, I put him on his defense on this very question. His only answer was to repeat his blunder. Thereupon Canon Girdlestone intervened to assure him that "he had been wholly misled by the English version," and the Duke of Argyll challenged his representation "both of the contention of Mr. Gladstone and the narrative in Genesis." My own rejoinder was to repeat his words in detail and to hold him to them.

Lawyers have a plea of "confession and avoidance"; Mr. Huxley's next letter was marked by avoidance without confession, and ended by a sneer at my reference to the spiritual side of Holy Scripture. To which the Duke of Argyll replied as follows:

> "In Professor Huxley's letter in your issue of yesterday he completely shifts his ground. He now asserts that Genesis ascribes creation to acts which he calls 'supernatural,' whereas, he urges, science asserts that it originated in a 'process of natural evolution.'

> "This antithesis is absolutely unknown to the literature both of the Old Testament and the New. It is equally unknown to science and also to philosophy. The Bible knows nothing of what men now call ' the supernatural.' It regards all 'natural processes' as the work of a Divine Being. Professor Huxley asserts or implies that this is erroneous, and that wherever we can trace the operation of natural causes, we must exclude all idea of a Divine origin or direction. I venture to assert, on the contrary, that this is very bad science, and still worse philosophy." (*The*

Chapter 9

Times, February 8, 1892. Mr. Huxley's letter here referred to is that which appeared in the Times of the 3rd, and which is reproduced in his Life (vol. 2, p. 297).)

The letter enlarges upon this, and ends by noting that the "broad issue" for which Mr. Huxley contended was, "that in ascribing the creative working to a Divine Being the narrative of Genesis is in 'irreconcilable antagonism' with modern science," an issue in which he would not have "the general support of the most eminent men of science in the United Kingdom."

My own final reply appeared in the same issue of *The Times*, as follows: —

> My rejoinder to Mr. Huxley shall be brief. Anyone who will be at the pains to turn to his Nineteenth Century articles will see that "his argument from Leviticus," instead of being, as he now pleads, "incidental" and "superfluous," was vital to his attack upon Mr. Gladstone's position. Upon it depended the only allegation of fact, as contrasted with theory, in his indictment of the Mosaic cosmogony. According to science reptiles existed before birds, but according to Genesis birds existed before reptiles. So he asserted. And the ground of his assertion was that, while birds belong to the fifth period of creation, "creeping things" belong to the sixth, and that "creeping things" are defined by "the Mosaic writer" himself in Leviticus 11. to include reptiles.
>
> Now that this is proved to be merely an *ad captandum* appeal to the phraseology of the English Bible, Mr. Huxley takes refuge in the plea that the word used in Genesis 1:24 may include reptiles. But this, even if true, will not help him. The fact remains that the word in Leviticus xi. is wholly different from the word used in Genesis 1:24, whereas the validity of his argument depends on its identity with it And the argument is his, not mine. He it is who insists that Genesis 1. must be interpreted by Leviticus 11; and, adopting his canon of interpretation, I have shown that he is "hoist with his own petard."

It is on petty points of this sort that the conventional attacks upon the Bible rest. But the foundations of faith are of a very different character. If facts be adduced to prove the Bible false, I shall give it up, and cease to be a Christian. But practical men and men of common sense care little for mere theories. In common with many other Christians I regard the Darwinian theory of evolution as being, within strictly defined limits, a reasonable hypothesis. But the peculiar biological theories with which Mr. Huxley's name is prominently identified, are in a different category. I am old enough to remember the time when they first gained currency in England. I am young enough to be warranted in hoping I may outlive their popularity. But these unproved, and possibly ephemeral, theories of the hour, dignified by the title of "natural science," are put forward as the grounds on which the Book of all the ages is to be rejected!

Mr. Huxley wrote another letter, but it contained nothing save pretentious phrases about science, and ungenerous sneers at those who believe the Bible. So far as this controversy is concerned he left his opponents in possession of the field. The fact asserted by Mr. Gladstone remains established by this searching test. It is asserted, and it will still be asserted as unblushingly as if this correspondence had not taken place, that Genesis is proved false by the facts of science; whereas the testimony of science, whatever it be worth, confirms the Biblical order of creation. [1] In *The Nineteenth Century* Mr. Huxley wrote, "There is no one to whose authority on geological questions I am more readily disposed to bow than that of my eminent friend Professor Dana;" and Professor Dana's decision was, "I agree in all essential points with Mr. Gladstone, and believe that the first chapter of Genesis and science are in accord."

> 1] And if any one now seeks to get rid of this by falling back on the "coincidence" theory, the mathematician will cut in to tell him that the order of any seven events can be given in no less than 5,040 ways.

For my part, I am willing to make the scientist a present of this conclusion. If Paleontology, instead of confirming, as it does, the Mosaic cosmogony, seemed to discredit it, the fact would only serve to strengthen the belief I entertain on independent grounds, that the fossils may be relics of an earlier economy of life, which was engulfed in the catastrophes which produced the present rock-formation of our earth.

Whether the origin of our globe was nebular or meteoric, it may have been the home of life for ages before the epoch of the Adamic creation. In the record of that creation the conception of a making-out-of-nothing has no place, The Bible is merely the history of the Adamic world, and even that, moreover, only as a background on which to display the great revelation of redemption. The opening verses of Genesis, therefore, mark the successive eras through which the Creator rescued our planet from its "waste and void" [1] condition, and prepared it as a fitting home for man; but as to its origin and earlier history Holy Writ is silent. "In the beginning God created the heaven and the earth." But when the beginning was, we cannot even conjecture; and if we go on to inquire the meaning of "creation," all that Scripture will tell us is that "things which are seen were not made of things which do appear" —a statement which will bear every test that can be applied to it. If in the past this earth ever suffered a catastrophe such as that which Scripture declares will engulf it in the future, the Mosaic narrative would be at once accounted for and explained.

> 1] Gen. 1:2. These same words are used in Jer. 4:23 of the ruin brought upon the land by the judgment of "the Desolations." That the earth was not originally "waste" Isa.45:18 declares.

That narrative is a part of the revelation upon which Christianity is based, and one essential portion of it—the recorded origin of the woman —is enshrined in the Christian system as typical of the spiritual union between Christ and His Church. I accept that narrative as a Divine revelation. And I endorse Mr. Huxley's dictum, "that it is vain to discuss a supposed coincidence between Genesis and science, unless we have first settled, on the one hand, what Genesis says, and, on the other hand, what science says." The matter is not ripe for discussion. We are a very long way indeed from settling "what science says"; and while it seems to be taken for granted that "what Genesis says" is known to all, closer study and fuller knowledge will destroy all dogmatism here.

When it is said that God "made the firmament," and the "two

great lights," and the "beasts of the earth," the same word is used as when Noah "made" the ark, and Moses the tabernacle. If abiogenesis [1] were an ascertained fact, and not an exploded error, the advocate of spontaneous generation might appeal to the language of the Creator's fiat, "Let the waters bring forth," "Let the earth bring forth." If evolution were an established truth, and not a mere theory, the evolutionist might turn to Genesis, and mark how order and life were slowly evolved in the world. Nor need he find any difficulty in supposing that mammals may have been developed among the "water population," and the "air population" too, before animals of that order appeared upon the land. Mr. Huxley's argument on this point is valid only as destroying the position to which his "Sunday-school exegesis" forced Mr. Gladstone to retreat.

> 1] A term coined by Huxley himself to express spontaneous generation.

I turn to the narrative. The earth existed, but it was "desolate and empty," a mere waste of waters, wrapped in impenetrable darkness. The changes recorded are, first, the dawn of light, and then the formation of an atmosphere followed by the retreat of the waters to their ocean bed; then the dry land became clothed with verdure, and sun and moon and stars appeared. [1]

> 1] The laughter formerly excited by the idea of light apart from the sun has died away with increasing knowledge (see Dr. Sinker's *Higher Criticism*, p. 121); and, in our ignorance of that primeval life, it is idle to question the possibility of the third-day vegetation. It may possibly have been the "rank and luxuriant herbage" of which our coal-beds have been formed; for one statement in the narrative seems strongly to favor the suggestion that our present vegetation dates only from the fifth or sixth day (Gen. 2:5, R.V.).

But the question remains, What was the creation day? No problem connected with the cosmogony has greater interest and importance. I own to a decided conviction that while the passage clearly indicates our ordinary day, the word is used in a purely symbolic sense. When dealing with a period before man existed to mark the shadow on the dial, and before the sun could cast that shadow, it is not easy to appreciate the reason, or indeed the meaning, of such a division of time as our natural day. "Days and years and seasons" seem plainly to belong to our present solar system, and this is the express teaching of the fourteenth verse. [1]

> 1] That the earth is older than the sun may at one time have appeared impossible. But it seems to be involved in the meteoric hypothesis.

The problem may be stated thus: As man is to God, so his day of four and twenty hours is to the Divine day of creation. And here I would suggest that the "evening and morning" may represent the interval of the cessation from work, which succeeds and completes the day. The words are, "And there was evening, and there was morning, one day." [1] The symbolism is maintained throughout. As man's working day is brought to a close by evening, which ushers in a period of repose, lasting till morning calls him back to his daily toil, so the great Artificer is represented as turning aside from His work at the end of each "day" of creation, and again resuming it when another morning dawned.

> 1] If the creation story was revealed by way of Apocalyptic visions, these words are fully explained.

And is not this in keeping with the mode in which Scripture speaks of God? It tells us of His mouth and eyes and nostrils, His hand and arm. It speaks of His sitting in the heavens, and bowing Himself to hear the prayer ascending from the earth. It talks of His repenting and being angry. And if one cavils at this, he may fairly be asked, In what other language could God speak to men?

Nor let anyone fall back on the common fallacy that a Divine day is a period of a thousand years. With God, we are told, a day is as a thousand years, and a thousand years as one day. In a word, the seeming paradox of the transcendental philosophy is endorsed by the express teaching of Scripture, that time is merely a law of human thought. When, therefore, God speaks of working for six days and resting on the seventh, we must understand the words in the same symbolic sense as when He declares that His hand has made all these things. [1]

> 1] Isa. 66:2.

But the mention of the creation Sabbath is the crowning proof of the symbolic character of the creation "day." God "rested on the seventh day from all the work which He had made." Are we, then, to suppose that He resumed the work when four and twenty hours had passed? Here, at least, revelation and science are at one: the creation Sabbath has continued during all the ages of historic time. God is active in His universe, pace the atheist and the infidel, but the Creator rests. Scripture, indeed, tells of a supreme catastrophe that is yet to engulf our planet, and of a new creation which is to follow it, of which the resurrection of Christ is the earnest and pledge. But these are topics I must not enter upon. I content myself with noticing the well-recognized fact that the creation Sabbath is a vast period of time, and urging that the working days of creation must be estimated on the same system.

This must be borne in mind as we proceed. The water population and the air population belong to the same "day"; but ages of time may have intervened before the appearance of the latter. [1] So also with the land population of the sixth day. For aught that we can tell, the appearance of man may have been separated from that of other mammals by a period of time as prolonged as that which divides the present hour from the close of the creation "week." [2]

> 1] Of course the suggestion of the Authorized Version is erroneous that the water was the birthplace of the "feathered tribe." The words are, "Let the waters bring forth abundantly the moving creature that hath life, and let fowl fly above the earth in the open firmament of heaven."

> 2] The second chapter indicates that there was an interval between the formation of the man and of the woman. The Paleontologists' proofs that earth was the dwelling-place of intelligent beings at a much earlier period, are not complete enough to justify any definite comparison between those earlier inhabitants and the Adamic race. Indeed, it is doubtful whether they afford certainty of being pre-Adamite at all.

But all this is mere conjecture. And my object in suggesting it is not to frame a system of interpretation, but to enter a caveat against confounding the teaching of Scripture with any system of interpretation whatever. I deprecate the idea that I am posing as a "reconciler." I have no such ambitious aim as that of seeking to convince the scientists. I wish rather to warn the faithful against assaults upon the Mosaic cosmogony, based on "the merest Sunday-school exegesis" on the one hand, and on the theories of science on the other. The facts of science in no way clash with Scripture. They serve only to assist us in understanding it aright.

Of the origin of our world the first chapter of Genesis tells us nothing, save that "in the beginning," whenever that was, God created it. It may be, as Mr. Tyndall said in his Belfast address, that "for aeons embracing untold millions of years, this earth has been the theatre of life and death." But as to this the Book of Genesis is silent. It deals merely with the renewing and refurnishing of our planet as a home for man. And this, moreover, as I have already urged, to prepare the foundation for the supreme revelation of redemption.

In conclusion, I would guard myself from any suspicion of seeking "to prove the truth of the Mosaic narrative." My object here is to beat off attacks which stumble or distress ignorant and weak-kneed believers. And to this end I have shown that Professor Huxley, the ablest and most bitter assailant of Genesis which this age has produced, has been met and routed upon ground of his own choosing. The first chapter of Genesis "was not written to teach science"; but not a single "fact of science" can be found to discredit it. This cannot be said of any one of "the religious books of the East" —in this respect they are but a tangle of error and folly. Neither can it be said of any scientific book published before recent years. The "science" of the last generation is discredited by the discoveries of our own times. Never until our own times have Scripture and science been in accord; but the changes which have harmonized them have been in science and not in Scripture. And this can only be explained on one of two hypotheses. Either science was more advanced when Genesis was written than at any time during all the Christian era, or else "the Mosaic narrative" is a Divine revelation. [1]

> 1] The Times correspondence quoted in this chapter originated with a "declaration on the truth of Holy Scripture," signed by Dean Goulbourn and a number of other clergymen, which appeared in The Times of December 18, 1891. My object in intervening was to point out that these clergymen in taking their stand upon the ground that the Church was "the witness and keeper of Holy Writ," betrayed the cause they sought to defend, and were false to

the Church of England, which in Article XX. claims only to be " a witness," etc. My second letter {*The Times*, January 23, 1892) was in reply to the letter of "A Beneficed English Clergyman of Twenty-five Years' Standing," who took infidel ground. Mr. Huxley's reply appeared in The Times of January 26th. Letters from the Duke of Argyll, Canon Girdlestone, and myself appeared on February 1st, and were answered by Mr. Huxley on February 3rd and 4th. My last letter (quoted above) appeared on February 8th, and Mr. Huxley's rejoinder on the nth. The title "The Bible and Modern Criticism" was assigned to the correspondence by the editor of *The Times*.

Chapter 10

More than a quarter of a century ago, when I first came definitely under the influence of the Higher Criticism, doubts began to undermine my faith in Holy Scripture. I then knew but little either of the history or the aims of the movement; and a taste for critical inquiries, combined with impatience of mere "orthodoxy," created in my mind a prejudice in its favor. At the same time I had a sufficient acquaintance with the general scheme of revelation, and especially with the typology and prophecy of Scripture, to prevent my being misled by the teaching of the critics about the Pentateuch, or by their theories that the "Priestly Code," as they call it, was later than the Prophets. This being so, it was not till I reached the Book of Daniel that I felt any serious alarm. The New Testament is so identified with that book (as the critics themselves allow) that if Daniel be discredited, the authority of the Gospels and Epistles is impaired, and the Apocalypse must be entirely given up. And yet the case against the book seemed overwhelming. Not only was its authenticity destroyed by glaring historical errors, but its claim to genuineness was vetoed by the very language in which it was written: its Hebrew, I learned, belonged to a later period than the Captivity, and the Greek words contained in it absolutely precluded an earlier origin than the date of Alexander's conquest.

Now, unlike the critics, my tenure of the public position I held was not conditioned upon any pledge that I believed the Scriptures. Had I come to accept the conclusions of the critics, I might have continued to draw the emoluments of my office without any twinges of conscience or any reflection upon my honor. When, therefore, I set myself to investigate the case against Daniel, I did so in the same spirit in which I have not infrequently prosecuted criminal charges against persons whom, though I greatly wished to save, I was determined to bring to justice if guilty. I say this because it is the fashion to assume that to attack the Bible gives proof not only of "culture," but of mental vigor and freedom, and that its defenders are always narrow-minded and prejudiced.

I first took up the special question upon which I was dependent upon the experts, namely, the philological features of the book. And here I kept to the writings of the critics. My first shock was the discovery that, according to the evidence of some of the most advanced and fearless of its assailants, the Hebrew of the book decides nothing as to its date. [1] The bold statements to the contrary, therefore, are proof only of recklessness on the part of those who make them.

> 1] See, e.g., Professor Cheyne's article "Daniel" in *Encyc. Brit.*

And my amazement and indignation reached a climax when I discovered that the supposed Greek words in Daniel had, one after another, been given up by the critics, until only two or three remained; and that it is upon these words, which are the names of musical instruments, that the critics veto the acceptance of the book. [1] If the instruments themselves came from Greece, it might be assumed that they would carry with them to Babylon the names by which they were known in the land of their origin. In no other sphere would men listen to what passes for proof when Scripture is assailed. In no other sphere would such trifling as this be tolerated. If only these men could be "got into court," and subjected to cross-examination, they would lose not only their case but their reputation!

> 1] Professor Driver of Oxford declares that "the Greek words demand, the Hebrew supports, and the Aramaic permits, a date after the conquest of Palestine by Alexander the Great" (*Book of Daniel*, p. 63). In the Introduction to Daniel in "The Temple Bible," Dr. Sinker writes: "Yet about this time a brother of the Greek poet Alcaeus held office at the Court of Babylon. Still earlier, Sargon mentions the Greeks (Javanu) of Cyprus; and much earlier, we find a Greek in the Tel-el-Amarna tablets. Clearly then there is no reason why in the time of Daniel Greek musical instruments and their names should not have been known in Babylon."

The argument from the language of the Book of Daniel having thus utterly broken down — in truth it is an insult to our intelligence

Chapter 10

—we dismiss the Philologists from the inquiry altogether. The remaining question is one of evidence of a wholly different kind; and no university professor, however eminent, is as fit to deal with it as the trained lawyer or the experienced juryman. I press this. These pages will be read by many who are as competent to decide the fate of Daniel as any of the critics whose dictum about the book is blindly accepted by the public. And those who study the controversy will recognize the truth of Hengstenberg's statement, that the attack upon the book originated in a prejudged determination to eliminate the supernatural element from the Bible. Devout men like Eichhorn and his pupil Ewald sought to win the rationalists back to religion by joining in their attack upon the only true basis of religion.

A criminal prosecution sometimes originates in some virulent prejudice which clouds the judgment even of fair and upright men. The Dreyfus case in France is the most famous example of this in modern times. No generous mind would tolerate the belief that men like the French Ministers of State were the guilty accessories to an infamous plot against an innocent man. They deprecated the methods of the prosecution, but they accepted the result. And so here, men like Professor Driver accept the verdict of the Higher Criticism against the Book of Daniel, while deprecating the "exaggerations of the rationalists." But whence these exaggerations? The Public Prosecutor does not "exaggerate" in presenting a case to the court. On the contrary he is careful to state it with perfect fairness, and to notice every point in favor of the accused as well as against him. Not so, however, a private prosecutor. The "exaggerations" of the German critics are the clearest proof that the crusade against Daniel was the outcome of prejudice or malice.

In my published defense of the book I have not sought to score a single point by trading on these "exaggerations." The popularity of the Dean of Canterbury precluded my ignoring him, but I have taken Professor Driver as the accredited exponent of the case of the English critics. And in meeting his indictment of Daniel, I have accepted his own statement of the evidence. Any competent tribunal would, I believe, decide that the Septuagint translation of the book is older than the date to which the critics assign the Hebrew original, and that the canon of the Old Testament was closed anterior to that date. But meeting them on their own ground, I have shown that no part of their case against the book will stand the test of cross-examination.

And further, it has been demonstrated that its great central prophecy has been fulfilled in Messianic times with absolute definiteness and precision. And this demonstration Professor Driver himself has cited, [1] only to leave it and pass on; though if it remains unchallenged it should end the controversy.

1] *Book of Daniel*, p. 149.

If there are those whose faith in Scripture depends on the fate of Daniel, a brief summary of the defense of the book may serve only to prejudice the issue. And yet the briefest summary is all that can be given within the limits of this chapter. [1]

1] Dean Farrar's philippic is a portly volume; and in Professor Driver's Book of Daniel the "Introduction" alone occupies a hundred closely printed pages. My reply to both occupies only a hundred and eighty pages of large and leaded type (*Daniel in the Critics' Den,* 1902). Greater condensation is impossible.

The critics' attack upon the book rests on three grounds: — philological peculiarities, historical errors, and its position in the canon. The first I have already dealt with. As regards the second, the only vital "error" is the opening statement of the book, that Nebuchadnezzar invaded Judea in the third year of Jehoiakim. But this is a fact in history established by writers sacred and profane.

The critics here rely on the history of Berosus, quoted by Josephus. That historian tells that during the expedition Nebuchadnezzar heard of his father's death, and at once handed over his Jewish captives to others, and "himself hastened home across the desert." The German rationalists, mixing up Berosus with Scripture, [1] and understanding neither, infer that it was from Carchemish, where a decisive battle was fought in the fourth year of Jehoiakim, that Nebuchadnezzar started homewards. But Carchemish is on the Upper Euphrates, and the road thence to Babylon is clear of the desert altogether. If, as Berosus tells us, Nebuchadnezzar had Jewish captives, he must have invaded Judea; and if the desert lay between him and his capital, it must have been from Judea that he set out on his homeward journey.

1] Jer. 46:2.

This "historical error" is a blunder so glaring that a schoolboy might well be ashamed of it. And yet it is gravely adopted and reproduced by English ecclesiastics and Professors for the enlightenment of a much deluded public. [1] It is a specimen of the "historical errors" of the Higher Critics. *Ex uno disce omnes.*

> 1] See Professor Driver's *Book of Daniel*, p. 2. Dean Farrar's words are: "Nor did Nebuchadnezzar advance against the Holy City even after the battle of Carchemish, but dashed home across the desert." One does not expect to be amused by a book on such a subject, but this is really amusing. The fact is these English scholars copy from the German rationalists without inquiry or independent thought. The refutation of this silly blunder does not depend merely on the point above mentioned, but upon the history as a whole. See *Daniel in the Critics' Den*, App. I.

Another "historical error" deserves a passing notice. When the skeptic s first framed their indictment of Daniel, Belshazzar appeared to be a myth. For history testifies that the last king of Babylon was Nabonidus; that he was absent from the capital when Cyrus entered it, and that he lived many years after the Persian conquest. The contradiction between history and Scripture was complete. But the since deciphered inscriptions have disclosed that Belshazzar was eldest son and heir to Nabonidus, that he was regent in Babylon during his father's absence, and that he was killed the night the Persian army entered the inner city. [1]

> 1] Professor Sayce's statements on this are but a false inference from a false reading of the tablet. See *Daniel in the Critics' Den*, App. II.

The only difficulty still unsolved in the Daniel story is the identity of Darius the Mede. But here again the inscriptions tell us that, in the conquest of Babylon, Cyrus had united with him a Median of such power and fame that it was he who appointed the new officials; and that when an amnesty was proclaimed, it was issued in their joint names. The absence of Darius's name from the commercial tablets is amply explained by the fact that, as Daniel indicates, he, like Belshazzar, was only a viceroy or vassal king.

Not one single new point against Daniel has been brought to light for a century. Every decade brings to light some new proofs of its genuineness and authenticity.

Daniel's place in the Canon is too large a question for incidental treatment. But the mere fact of its inclusion would satisfy any fair tribunal of the genuineness of the book, and it renders it absolutely certain that the Sanhedrim regarded it as genuine.1 In the Septuagint version, moreover, it is placed among the prophets, as in our English Bible; which seems to indicate that such was its original position. And if so its transfer to the third division of the Canon was effected, no doubt, after the beginning of the Christian era. The Hebrew Bible now brackets it with the Psalms of David and other books held by the Jews in the very highest esteem.

Then, again, the critics cannot tear from its pages the great prophecy of the "Seventy Weeks." And that prophecy, so far as its fulfilment belongs to the past, was fulfilled with such definiteness and precision as to make an "end of controversy" upon the whole question. Taking history from the historian and chronology from the chronologist, it will be found that the interval from the issue of the decree to build Jerusalem to the public proclamation of the Messiah, was exactly and to the very day the period foretold by Daniel. [1]

1] See *Daniel in the Critics' Den*, pp. 99-111.

Could the prediction have been a mere guess by some learned and pious Jew? If we refer this question to a mathematician he will tell us that in such a forecast the chance of accuracy would be so small, and the probability of error so great, that neither the one nor the other could be expressed arithmetically in figures. The calculation, in fact, would become lost in infinity. The attempt, therefore, to dismiss the fulfilment of the prophecy as a mere coincidence "is not intelligent skepticism, but a crass misbelief which is sheer credulity."

And lastly the fact claims notice — and this alone should satisfy the Christian—that the Book of Daniel bears the express imprimatur of our Divine Lord. Witness His words: "When ye, therefore, shall see the abomination of desolation, spoken of by Daniel the prophet, stand in the holy place." The attempt to evade this by the plea that the words here given in italics are a gloss, is so unwarranted that no English writers would have suggested it were it not that they follow the German skeptic s like sheep. The words occur in the great prophecy of Matthew 24; and the reference to Daniel is so unmistakable that the omission of the name could not even obscure it.

Chapter 10

1] According to Dan. 9:25, sixty-nine sevens of prophetic years were to elapse between the issuing of the edict to rebuild the city, and "Messiah the Prince"; and the period from 1st Nisan in the 20th year of Artaxerxes (Neh. 2) to "Palm Sunday" when our Lord made His public entry into Jerusalem (Luke 19:36-38) was exactly 173,880 days (=69 x 7 x 360). This is dealt with in detail in *The Coming Prince*, and also in *Daniel in the Critics' Den* (1902).

Bishop Westcott declares that "no other book of the Old Testament had so great a share in the development of Christianity." It is Hengstenberg's testimony that "there are few books whose Divine authority is so fully established by the testimony of the New Testament, and in particular by the Lord Himself." And even Professor Bevan of Cambridge —one of the narrowest of the critics —admits that "the influence of the book is apparent almost everywhere."

But the Christian accepts the Book, not because its rejection would be, as Sir Isaac Newton urged, "to undermine the Christian religion"; but because its claims to acceptance are complete and convincing, and the case for its rejection owes its seeming cogency only to ignoring some of the most salient facts, and misrepresenting others.

1] In reading this chapter in the proof I am increasingly impressed with its inadequacy as a defense of Daniel; especially as I have so very recently (Easter, 1902) published my full answer to the indictment as formulated by Professor Driver and Dean Farrar. In *Daniel in the Critics' Den* (1902) not a single point urged by the assailants is overlooked, and the critics are put upon their defense. I have only now had the benefit of reading the "Introduction" and Notes to Daniel in *The Temple Bible*.

Chapter 11

Among the many stories told of Chief Baron O'Grady, first Lord Guillamore, of the Irish Court of Exchequer, there is one about a judgment of his which is probably unique in judicial annals. The two judge Barons who were sitting with him in bank in the hearing of an important case, had delivered elaborate judgments, taking opposing views of the law; and the Chief Baron's judgment which followed was given in the single sentence, "I agree with my brother Smith for the reasons assigned by my brother McClelland."

When the mind is wavering in its acceptance of what seems to be true and right, there is nothing so helpful as an able and exhaustive statement of all that can be said upon the other side. In this way I owe much to the Higher Critics for settling my faith in Scripture; and I confess that my full acceptance of the Book of Jonah dates from my study of their reasons for rejecting it.

We all know the old woman who was ready to believe that Jonah swallowed the whale, if only the Bible said so; but we are not all equal to faith feats of that kind. From standard books of great authority I learned that it would be as impossible for a whale to swallow a man as for a man to swallow a whale; the shark was said to be the only fish in the sea that could accomplish it; and my faith became somewhat knock-kneed in presence of the shark. [1]

> 1] I am not justifying my skepticism. For the word translated "whale" in our New Testament may mean any large fish. But our minds easily become enslaved not only to ideas but to words.

But I was reminded of the words, "Now the Lord had prepared a great fish to swallow up Jonah." Yes, there is no doubt that Almighty God could extemporize a sea monster for the purpose. And such a miracle would not involve a greater display of power than many others ; but it would be a miracle of a kind that has no precedent or analogy in Scripture. We have learned to re-define "supernatural power"; for "nature" is merely a way of expressing one sphere of God's working. And as already noticed, Divine miracles are wholly free from any merely dramatic display of the resources of the Almighty. My difficulty therefore was, not that what was narrated was supernatural, but that it seemed natural.

And yet the fact was indisputable that nothing in the Old Testament was accredited more definitely by the Lord Jesus Christ than this very miracle. It was used by Him not as an incidental illustration, but as a prophecy and a type in the strictest sense, of His death and resurrection. There is no evading this; and therefore the Christian will find that to jettison the prophet Jonah, so far from calming the waves of skepticism, will only bring the barque of his faith into still greater peril.

We have become accustomed to find that distinguished Professors, and ecclesiastics of high degree, in criticizing the Bible, sometimes display ignorance of spiritual things; but in the sphere of the natural one does expect facts from their lips and pens. A friend of mine put up a new summerhouse in his garden. The entrance to it is so wide that a carriage and pair might drive through it; and that entrance consists of the jaws of a sperm whale!

A whale unable to swallow a man! In his Cruise of the "Cachelot," Mr. Bullen, an experienced whale fisher himself, describes the creature's mouth as large enough to hold a picnic party, and he tells of a shark 15 feet long being found in the stomach of one of these monsters. A whale that he himself helped to kill ejected the food it had swallowed; and it was, he says, "in masses of enormous size, some of them being estimated to be of the size of our hatch-house, viz., 8 feet x 6 feet x 6 feet." And in this connection he mentions a fact of special interest here, that the whale when dying vomits the contents of its stomach.

This same writer discusses the question how a monster so unwieldy can get hold of the smaller fish. "It is manifestly absurd," he says, "to suppose the whale capable of catching fish in the ordinary sense, indicating pursuit." And his explanation of it is that "as the cachelot [whale] swims about with his lower jaw hanging down in its normal position, and his huge gullet gaping like a submarine cavern, the fish unwittingly glide down it."

When in the light of these facts I again take up the Book of Jonah, I am conscious of a strange revulsion of feeling. The Hebrew Concordance tells me that when I read that "God prepared a great fish," the word used is the same as when the king of Babylon "appointed" a certain provision for Daniel and his companions. In other words, the statement means that in the providence of God, when Jonah was thrown overboard, one of these huge sea monsters was swimming by, "his huge gullet gaping like a submarine cavern," and Jonah went down just as a midge might go down the throat of a man when running against the wind.

This part of the miracle, therefore, which I was inclined to reject as being unprecedented and unnatural, proves to be no miracle at all. Neither is there any miracle in Jonah's being vomited out again: that was a process as natural as for a child to get rid of its dinner. Both the swallowing and the vomiting were perfectly natural, and there was nothing about either to excite even our wonder, much less incredulity. Where the miracle began and ended was that God preserved the life of His servant through it all.

And here —to repeat a favorite phrase —faith and unbelief must measure their distance. To say that God could not do this is to deny God altogether: to say He would not do it is absurd —any one of us would do it in similar circumstances if only we had the power: to say He did not do it is a flagrant case of begging the question. The New Testament refers to Jonah as a prophecy of the resurrection of Christ. For "He rose again the third day according to the Scriptures"; [1] and where, save in Jonah, shall we find in the Old Testament a plain and clear prophecy of His rising on the third day? And the Lord Jesus Christ, in the most definite and solemn manner, identified Himself with this very miracle. In the beginning of His ministry "signs " abounded; but when, after the Council which decreed His rejection, the Pharisees again demanded a "sign," His answer was that the only sign they should have was "the sign of the prophet Jonah." His words, repeated we know not how often, cannot be explained away: — "As Jonah was three days and three nights in the whale's belly, so shall the Son of Man be three days and three nights in the heart of the earth." [2] Some people seem to classify the miracles of Scripture. The little miracles they accept as a matter of course: it is only the big ones which try their faith. I would suggest to such people to enter the Jonah miracle low down on their list, but at the top to place those most stupendous and seemingly incredible of all miracles, the incarnation and resurrection of the Lord Jesus Christ. And when in some little measure they have realized who and what He is, His words will silence unbelief; and they will recognize that whatever judgment may be formed upon the Book of Jonah, the miracle which it records is inseparably identified with the truth of Christianity.

> 1] Cor. 15:4 (see above).
>
> 1] Matt 12:38-40, and 16:4. The Lord may have given the same answer a score of times for aught we know. And see above, and Appendix, Note III.

That it was on account of the miracle that the Germans decreed the rejection of the Book no honest person would dispute. But after their manner, they heaped up incidental reasons for their decision. And these reasons their English followers have, with childlike simplicity, adopted. Their interpretation is of the nightmare kind; everything in the book ought to have happened differently; things are included which ought to have been omitted, and things are omitted which ought to have been included. The only element of doubt is whether it is typical, or mythical, or legendary, or allegorical. Historical it certainly cannot be.

Now this sort of criticism any Old Bailey practitioner could work up far better than the Professors. For let it be kept in view that the whole argument from the language of the Book may be ruled out. Professor Driver indeed asserts that "It cannot have been written until long after the time of Jonah." But this is only Professor Driver's way. Even such an uncompromising critic as Professor Cheyne dissociates himself from such a conclusion; [1] and as anyone can see, the grounds set out in support of it are entirely inadequate. And this being so, we may dismiss the Hebraists from the inquiry, and consider the general question on its merits.

> 1] He somewhat superciliously remarks, "The evidences of date are difficult to seize" (*Encyclopedia Britannica*, article "Jonah"). And see *Speaker's Commentary*, "Jonah," Excursus B; and also the late Dr. John Kennedy's valuable monograph On the Book of Jonah (chap. 8).

Though Professor Driver denies the genuineness of the book, he is careful, as usual, to dissociate himself from the reckless extremes of the more advanced critics. "No doubt," he says, "the outlines of the narrative are historical." And yet "there are indications that it is not strictly historical." [1] These "indications" are:

That the conversion of the Ninevites is "contrary to analogy."

That such a conversion "should have produced so little permanent effect."

That it is not "easy to imagine" the king acting as is represented.

1] Introduction, "Jonah."

This, remember, represents the superior enlightenment and intelligence of the Higher Criticism. Of the king referred to we know nothing; and possibly if his character were known it would not be "easy to imagine" his acting in any other way! And as regards the second point, it is only a student among his books, who knows nothing practically of human nature, who could entertain such an objection. I put it on this ground because it is idle to appeal to the history of the chosen people in the wilderness, for these critics dismiss the divinely given story as a legend. But the repentance of the Ninevites is "contrary to analogy." Yes, and the conduct of masses of men when moved by any powerful passion is generally "contrary to analogy."

But there is something else which, if we extend our view beyond our own times, is also contrary to analogy; and that is that any man holding the position of an English clergyman should treat with such entire indifference the words of his Divine Lord. "The men of Nineveh shall rise in judgment with this generation, and shall condemn it; because they repented at the preaching of Jonah; and, behold, a greater than Jonah is here." [1] Let the critics, dealing with the studies which alone are within their competence, give us reasons to doubt the genuineness of the Book of Jonah, and we will consider the question on its merits. But that the men of Nineveh repented at the preaching of Jonah is a fact which rests, not on the Book of Jonah merely, but on the word of "a greater than Jonah"—the Lord Jesus Christ Himself.

1] Matt 12:41.

Chapter 11

The view of the Book presented by these writers is but a grotesque travesty. We seem to see a dripping, half-drowned Jew rushing through Nineveh, and shouting his startling message, like an escaped lunatic turned town-crier. And presto! all the inhabitants repent and turn good like clockwork, while the prophet himself turns sulky and bolts. This is their reading of it. This is Higher Criticism!

"Oh, the blindness of conventional critics, groping in Hebrew records not for pearls of facts, but for pebbles of dogma! They have failed to observe that the God of Jonah is the God of the New Testament. Yet it is so, and this great book connects the two Bibles, instead of contrasting them." [1]

> 1] The words are from the pen of Charles Reade. He declares that this Book of "1,328 English words" "is the most beautiful story ever written in so small a compass" {Bible Characters).

The Book is essentially a drama, of which the brief and quickly changing scenes present a story that is wonderfully real and intensely human. Can men who scout the idea of a prophet's refusing a call to service, and fleeing from the Lord, know anything of the deeper experiences of a spiritual life? And in such cases the Divine action is generally "contrary to analogy." When Paul was bidden to go to Rome, and yet turned to Jerusalem, he was brought to Rome as a prisoner, discredited by a chain: when Jonah was bidden to go to Nineveh, and yet took ship for Tarshish, he ended by entering Nineveh as a prophet accredited by a miracle. For the fame of his miraculous deliverance preceded him [1]; and when he proclaimed that the God by whom he had been thus delivered had decreed the destruction of their city, all men naturally hung upon his words. What calls to righteousness he uttered upon that wonderful text during the forty days of his ministry we know not. We can only conjecture what such preaching must have been.

> 1] The Lord's words in Luke 11:30 admit of no other meaning. He Himself as crucified and risen was to be "a sign" to Israel, just as Jonah rescued from death was a sign to the Ninevites.

And when the forty days were expired, he left the capital and made a hermit's lodge in which to wait "till he might see what would become of the city." But the days went by and nothing whatever happened. There must have been critics and skeptics in plenty in a place like Nineveh, and we can well imagine how they crowed. The men of faith, the "overcomers," are "a little flock" in every age; with the many the prophet and the prophet's God must soon have become a byword and a jest. And we can realize how Jonah would murmur against God, even as Elijah did, and, like him, exclaim, "I have been very jealous for the Lord God of hosts."

Every Christian who knows what it is to have a spiritual history has in some little measure had such experiences as these. And then it is that a silent heaven crushes us; then it is that the heart craves some token of the Divine presence. And we can imagine with what gladness Jonah recognized such a token in the gourd raised up to shelter him. We can imagine, too, the bitterness of the recoil when the vulgar facts of a waking day—the east wind and the garish sunshine—destroyed his gourd and threw him back upon himself. And as the curtain falls upon this last scene we almost seem to hear the closing words, "Thou hast had pity on the gourd, for which thou hast not labored, neither made it to grow; which came up in a night and perished in a night. And should not I spare Nineveh, that great city, wherein are more than six score thousand persons that cannot discern between their right hand and their left?"

Chapter 12

What I am about to narrate may well appear so incredible that I am prepared to find that my personal guarantee of its truth will at first sight fail to carry conviction.

A few years ago —I could give details of every part of my narrative —a certain London merchant killed an unfortunate wretch whom circumstances had placed in his power. He did not actually kill him with his own hands, but he had him brought to a secluded room which was deliberately prepared for the purpose, and there he stood by while his victim was strangled by a man whom he had hired to do the deed. I myself examined the place. I can testify, moreover, that all the facts were known, not only to the authorities, but to the Queen. And yet not only did the homicide go unpunished, but, with full knowledge of all I have narrated, Her Majesty singled him out for royal favor and conferred a title upon him.

What estimate will my readers form of such conduct on the part of one whom we have been taught to regard as a pattern and paragon of public and private virtue?

But before they pass judgment upon the facts they ought to know a few additional details. The victim of the tragedy I have described was a condemned murderer; the man who was paid to strangle him was the common hangman, the secluded room was in Newgate prison, and the merchant who received a knighthood was the Sheriff whose official duty it was to execute the criminal.

And now the meaning of my parable will begin to dawn upon the reader. Let these added details be suppressed, and a plain narrative which does not contain a syllable that is untrue or even exaggerated, may seem to endanger the reputation of Queen Victoria. And it is precisely by this sort of suppression that the Bible and the God of the Bible are misrepresented. Will any "person of culture" in our day dare to defend the extermination of the Canaanites? Will any one, I answer, dare to defend the strangling of a poor helpless wretch in a shut-in room?

It is not God's way to justify Himself at the bar of His creature's judgment. He acts and speaks autocratically. But in this matter He has deigned to explain His decrees. Men read the Bible story in the false light of the evolution craze. They picture to themselves a number of semi-civilized tribes on the upward path of progress, exterminated by an invading horde of religious fanatics. [1] But the Christian knows that they were a degenerate and apostate race whose destruction was decreed by a God of infinite mercy, because they had given themselves up to unnatural and loathsome sin. Four centuries had passed since Sodom fell. And among the citizens of Sodom not even ten could be found who were clear of the evil. What then must have been the condition of the land when God at last called in the Israelites as His executioners? Of the guilty nations there was one that seemed still to merit pity, and on account of that nation the judgment was delayed. If for four generations the favored people were left as strangers in a strange land, it was "because the iniquity of the Amorites was not yet full." [2]

> 1] The discoveries of the archeologist make it plain that at the era of the Exodus, Palestine had long enjoyed a high civilization (*Lex Mosaica*, p. 9). The nations were lapsing from civilization, not emerging from barbarism.
>
> 2] Gen.15:16, and see 13:15 and 18:32, and compare Rom. 1:21 ff. This is not a subject for plain speaking. I will dismiss it with the strange confession that prior to knowledge acquired at Scotland Yard, these Divine judgments upon Canaan were a difficulty to my faith. There are some kinds of vice that seem to spread like leprosy, and to become hereditary.

Considering that the historic Church of Western Christendom, by disparaging the sacred bond of marriage, affects a higher standard of morality than the Divine revelation of Christianity will sanction, it is not strange that men should claim to be more merciful than God. But the Bible narrative makes it clear as light that the extermination of the Canaanites was the carrying out of a Divine decree. That the men of a wandering tribe, with neither cavalry nor "military base," and encumbered by multitudes of women and children and camp followers, should conquer a nation with walled towns and "chariots of iron" —the equivalent of modern artillery —this is a feat to which history affords no parallel. And seven such nations fell before the Israelite invaders. Such facts seem to indicate that it was as clearly a Divine judgment as was the destruction of Pharaoh's army in the sea.

To the solution of other "difficulties" of a kindred type my parable may afford the clue; as, for example, the imprecatory Messianic Psalms, which are prophetic warnings of Divine judgments upon those who take the place of enemies of God. But I turn away to notice briefly difficulties of another kind, which depend, not on ignoring facts, but on perverting them. I will select one as illustrating the class to which I refer. What can be more unlike the Christian's God than the scheme of granting to the Jews a monopoly of Divine favor, and leaving the world to its fate? To which I will make answer by asking another question, *What can be more unlike the Christian's Bible?*

In commerce there are two well-known systems on which merchants deal with the public. The one is to sell directly to everyone who wishes to become a customer ; the other is to deal only through an agent. When the owner of some famous French vineyard, for instance, appoints an English agent, and refuses to supply his wines except through that agent, his object is to make it easier for the English public to obtain supplies, and to ensure them against adulteration and fraud. And God's purpose for Israel was that that favored nation should be His agents upon earth. Jerusalem was to be "the place of His name." But "the house of God," designed to become a house of prayer for all nations, they treated as their own, and ended by making it "a den of thieves." [1]

1] Kings 8: 41-43; Isaiah 66:7; Mark 11:17 (R.V.).

All nations are to be blessed in Christ; and the Israelites as a people were a type of Christ, and ought to have been a blessing to the world. But instead of bringing honor to the name of God, they caused His name to be blasphemed among the heathen. [1] They were as false to the Divine trust committed to them, as the "historic Church" of Christendom has been in this Christian dispensation.

1] Rom. 2: 24; Ezek. 36:20, 23.

In cases of this kind human error either ousts Divine truth altogether, or else becomes so identified with it in popular estimation that men in rejecting the error reject also the truth. And in this respect very "superior persons" are often the greatest offenders. Matthew Arnold, for instance, like many another writer of the same type, identifies the truth of the Eden fall with that horror of Augustinian theology, the damnation of infants. [1] Indeed the whole Augustinian doctrine of election, as distinguished from the truth of election, is a case of putting the new wine of the Christian revelation into the old bottles of a bygone dispensation.

1] See p. 219, post.

I will here notice, in passing, a Biblical "blunder" of which much has been made. In 2 Sam. 24:24, we read that David bought the oxen and threshingfloor of Araunah for fifty shekels of silver. From 1 Chron. 21:25, we learn that David gave 600 shekels of gold for the place. It is extraordinary that any honest and intelligent mind could find a difficulty here. Fifty shekels of silver were presumably a fair price, though to us it seems very little, for the oxen and for the temporary use of the threshingfloor, for the purpose of the sacrifice. [1] And this was all that the king had in view at the moment. But does anyone imagine that the fee-simple of "the place" —the entire site of the Temple — was worth only fifty silver shekels? David went on to purchase the entire homestead out and out; and the price he paid for it was 600 shekels of gold. And this is what the "Chronicler" records.

> 1] The English reader must not base anything on the force of the English words "buy" and " bought" in 2 Sam. xxiv. 24. The narrative in Chronicles suggests that it was the Lord's "answering him by fire" that led the king to go on to the purchase of the place.

The "Chronological errors" of the Bible fall within the same category. Mere textual blunders seem scarcely worth notice here, such, e.g., as the reading seven instead of three in 2 Sam. 24:13, [1] and eight instead of eighteen in 2 Chron. 36:9. Having regard to all the circumstances, the wonder is that such mistakes are so rare. But the whole scheme of Biblical chronology is regarded as proof of error. This will repay looking into.

> 1] The LXX reads *three*, and this in itself proves that it is merely an error of copying.

No skeptic will accept the wild chronology of the Egyptologists. If the English people were not so unimaginative, they would reckon the several dynasties of the Heptarchy as successive, and thus lay claim to a really imposing national antiquity. But no one who has studied the subject will dispute that the story of man's tenancy of the earth reaches back to an earlier period than Biblical chronology appears to warrant. Such a discovery, however, troubles only those who suppose the Bible to be a history of the human race. [1]

> 1] See p. 194, post.

Upon this subject the intelligent Bible student will not fail to arrive at three conclusions. The first is that there is a definite system in Biblical chronology; and the second is that the writers had no thought of any system whatever. And, thirdly, finding that there is a system, and that it is not the outcome of human thought or plan, he will accept the obvious conclusion that it is Divine.

Some of our chronologists have vaguely noticed such a system, but all of them have been misled by the universally prevailing error of regarding the birth of Christ, and not the Crucifixion, as the crisis and close of the Jewish dispensation. As to His birth date Scripture is silent; but His death date is fixed with definiteness. For no date in history is indicated more precisely than the epoch of the Ministry, namely, the 15th year of Tiberius Caesar; and as the Crucifixion occurred at the fourth Passover of the Ministry, its date is definitely fixed by Scripture itself as in A.D. 32. [1]

> 1] Luke 3:1 is an end of controversy on this subject with all who reject the nightmare system of interpreting Scripture. The matter is fully discussed in *Daniel in the Critics' Den*, App. 6, and also in *The Coming Prince*, to which I beg to refer the reader.

On a subject of this kind all heresies and fads are to be deprecated. Let us accept the dates as given by our greatest chronologist, Fynes Clinton. But with one slight correction. His "Adam" date is B.C. 4138, and his "Deluge" date 2482; but for cogent reasons given by the learned author of the *Ordo saeclorum*, I would add three years to the Gen. 12-14 period, and fix the Creation at B.C. 4141, and the Deluge at B.C. 2485. Clinton assigns the Call of Abraham to B.C. 2055, and the Exodus to B.C. 1625.

Clinton fixed these several dates without reference to any system; but their striking significance will be made clear by the following table: —

B.C.

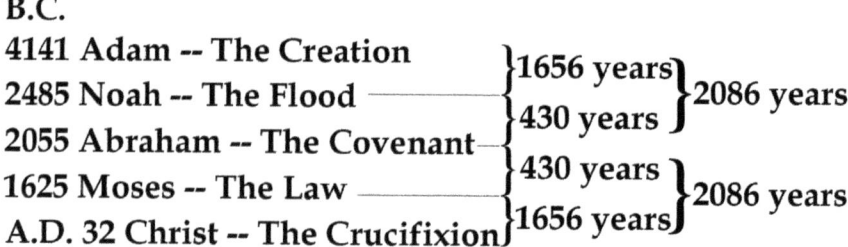

Now to dismiss these results as accidental is simply absurd. Certain it is that they are absolutely accidental in the sense that they were not designed either by the chronologist or by the "Biblical writers." But the proof these figures afford of a Divine plan of "time and seasons" is overwhelming. And if anyone should still insist that the results are a mere coincidence, the mathematician will tell him that the probabilities against such a coincidence are altogether incalculable. In a word, such a conclusion is a misbelief which revolts our intelligence.

Are we, then, to conclude that the period from this "Coronation year," 1902, to the first appearance of the Adam race on earth was exactly 6,042 years? By no means. Scripture itself will furnish us with a clue to the system on which the Divine chronology is framed.

According to 1 Kings 6:1, Solomon's temple was begun in the 480th year from the Exodus. "If a little of the time and energy which the critics have expended in denouncing that passage as a forgery or a blunder had been devoted to searching for its hidden meaning, their labors might perchance have been rewarded. That the chronology of the period was known is plain from Acts 13, which enables us to reckon the very same era as 573 years. How then can this seeming error of 93 years be accounted for? It is precisely the sum of the several eras of the Servitudes. The inference, therefore, is clear that 'the 480th year' means the 480th year of national life and national responsibilities." [1]

1] Acts 13:18-21 gives 40 years in the wilderness, 450 years under the Judges, and 40 years for the reign of Saul. To which must be added the 40 years of David's reign, and the first three years of Solomon, for it was in his fourth year that he began to build the Temple. The servitudes were to Mesopotamia for 8 years, to Moab for 18 years, to Canaan for 20 years, to Midian for 7 years, and to the Philistines for 40 years. See Judges 3:8, 14; 4:2, 3; 6:1; 13:1. But 8 + 18 + 20-1-7 + 40 years are precisely equal to 93 years. To believe that this is a mere coincidence would involve an undue strain upon our faith.

Acts 13:20 is one of the very many passages where the New Testament Revisers have corrupted the text through neglect of the well-known principles by which experts are guided in dealing with conflicting evidence. It is certain that neither the apostle said, nor the evangelist wrote, that Israel's enjoyment of the land was limited to 450 years, or that 450 years elapsed before the era of the Judges. The text adopted by R.V. is therefore clearly wrong. Dean Alford regards it "as an attempt at correcting the difficult chronology of the verse;" and he adds, "taking the words as they stand, no other sense can be given to them than that the time of the Judges lasted 450 years." That is, as he explains, not that the Judges ruled for 450 years—in which case the accusative would be used, as in verse 18—but, as the use of the dative implies, that the period until Saul, characterized by the rule of the Judges, lasted 450 years.

The objection that I omit the servitude of Judges 10:7, 8 is met by a reference to the R.V. The punctuation of the passage in Bagster's Bible perverts the sense. That servitude affected only the tribes beyond Jordan.

Call this a coincidence, and the mathematician will tell you again that the probabilities against such a coincidence are simply incalculable. When the rejection of one hypothesis involves the acceptance of another, mere unbelief degenerates into misbelief.

A life without God is death. Righteousness must keep a strict account, or Grace may pardon. And when God forgives sin, He "remembers it no more." The record is wiped out, and the time it covers is treated as a blank. The days of our servitude to sin are ignored in the Divine chronology. May not this be the explanation of the enigma? And if it be, we shall be prepared to find that possibly the Divine chronology of the race omits as many periods of various lengths as does the 480 years era of 1 Kings 6.

But this is mere conjecture. What concerns us is the fact, first, that the chronology of the Old Testament is framed upon a system, and a system, moreover, which is not of human design; and secondly, that there is a mystic element in it. And if when the Egyptologists have been brought to reason by some process akin to "cross-examination," it should become clear that the history of our race extends back far beyond the time of which Scripture appears to take cognizance, the discrepancy may be thus accounted for.

The element of design is beyond question, and the clue to it is to be found in the history of the favored people. As we have seen, the covenant with Abraham is made the central date between the Creation and the Cross, and the ages measured back and forward from that epoch are each divided into two periods of equal length, but in inverse order. And the history of that people is marked throughout by cycles of "seventy weeks" of years.

From the entrance into Canaan (B.C. 1586-5) to the establishment of the monarchy (B.C. 1096) was 490 years.

From the kingdom (B.C. 1096) to the Servitude to Babylon (B.C. 606) was 490 years.

From the conquest by Babylon the national history of Judah was suspended until the royal edict of Artaxerxes Longimanus of Persia ordered the rebuilding of the walls of Jerusalem, and restored the old polity of the Judges; and then began the mystic era of 490 years which constitute the "seventy weeks" of Daniel's prophecy.

And from the dedication of Solomon's temple (B.C. 1005) to the dedication of the second temple in the sixth year of Darius Hystaspis (B.C. 515) was also a period of 490 years.

Now all this is deduced from works written in different ages by men who had no plan or purpose of the kind in view. To attribute the results to chance is too silly for discussion, and no intelligent person will hesitate to conclude that the chronology of the Old Testament is part of a Divine plan, or "economy of times and seasons." I deprecate the suggestion that the Christian's faith in the Bible depends on such incidental proofs of its "hidden harmony." But they are not altogether without value as an antidote to the skepticism of the critics.

Chapter 13

I have a vivid recollection of a conversation it was my privilege to hold some years ago with one whose words, whether by voice or pen, always command the attention of the public, and who has identified himself to some extent with the Higher Criticism. He took exception to my saying that the truth of Christianity is identified with the Divine authority of the Hebrew Scriptures. The teaching of the Lord Himself, he averred, was its full and sufficient basis; and for that teaching we are dependent only on the Gospels. And on my pressing him he maintained that the Gospels were inspired in a special sense —in the strictest sense, indeed, in which both Jews and Christians have spoken of inspiration— so that even in such prolonged discourses as "the Sermon on the Mount," we have an infallible record of the very words of Christ.

"But," I urged, "if you accept the inspiration of the Gospels — and the denial of it destroys the only reasonable foundation for our faith in Christ —you must accept also the Lord's teaching as to the Divine authority of the Old Testament. You want me to believe, moreover, that the Gospel of Luke, for example, is fully and strictly inspired, but that the Acts, written by the same Evangelist, is of lower authority and value; and that the Epistles, though written by inspired Apostles, were not inspired in the same sense as the Gospels, two of which are by men who were not apostles at all."

To this I received no answer. Nor is any answer possible. Every free and fearless thinker will side with me in saying that no compromise of the kind thus proposed is tenable. We must make choice between two positions in this matter. Either the Bible is "God-breathed" (which is the traditional belief of the people of God in all ages), or else its claim to our faith is merely that it consists in the main of the writings of men who received Divine revelations, and therefore that it contains such revelations. Or to state the problem in other words, either the Bible is the Word of God, or it merely contains portions and truths which may in a sense be thus described.

And the question here involved is not affected by doubts as to the genuineness of some particular book or books. If an expert examines the contents of my purse and convinces me that one of my coins is spurious, the discovery only serves to give me increased confidence in the value of the rest. This is not in the least what people usually mean who say that the Bible merely contains the Word of God. They mean that the human element so permeates the mass that no part of it is absolutely Divine. The Divine element, therefore, which is also present, and on account of which they maintain in a sense the Inspiration of the Scriptures, is no guarantee of absolute truth. In fact they give to the word Inspiration "a meaning which is in great measure independent of the truth or falsehood of the writings so inspired." [1]

1] Prebendary Wace, D.D., *Lex Mosaica*, p. 610.

Now any person of ordinary intelligence can see that a Bible of this kind affords no ground for faith. We may say "I think," "I hope;" but to go on and say "I believe," "I know," would be unwarrantable. This does not trouble the mere library student; but those who are actively engaged in the Christian ministry, and have practical acquaintance with the spiritual needs of men, know well that this half skepticism will not satisfy any who are alive to the great realities of "sin and righteousness and judgment." For nothing short of certainty will satisfy the awakened soul.

Until recent years, in Britain at least, certainty was found in the Bible regarded as Divinely inspired; and here it was that faith and unbelief measured their distance. But it is a notable test of the growth of "the Christian religion" and the decline of Christianity, that so many of those who give up the Bible are eager to claim a footing in the camp of faith. The compromise which satisfies some is that to which I have referred, the setting up an inner Canon within the Canon of Scripture, by arbitrarily selecting certain books as being in a special sense inspired. But this, as we have seen, is not even consistent with itself.

The *Lux Mundi* school, on the other hand, has fallen back on "the Church" as the source of authority. In this matter the position of the Church of Rome is that of the Latin fathers in the teaching of the fourth and fifth centuries. It was definitely formulated by Augustine of Hippo, according to whom, as Professor Harnack puts it, "The

Church guaranteed the truth of the faith, when the individual could not perceive it." But behind the Church was an inspired, and therefore infallible, Bible, of which it was the Divinely appointed custodian. [1] Now this position is at least intelligent, and it may be stated in a way that seems to command approval. Our Courts of Justice are not above the law, but they are the accredited exponents of the law; and it rests with them, and not with private persons, to interpret the law. And so here, the Church does not claim to supplant the Bible, but merely to interpret it authoritatively and infallibly.

> 1] This is reaffirmed in that wonderful document, the Pope's Encyclical letter of November 18, 1893.

And this was, with certain modifications, the position maintained by English High Churchmen of the last generation. But the new school of which the editor of *Lux Mundi* is the apostle, sets up the Church, not because the private Christian is incompetent to interpret the infallible Bible, but because the Bible, so far from being infallible, is marred by error, and therefore affords no sure basis of faith.

> The ancient theory is thus described by Professor Huxley in his last letter in the Times correspondence cited in chapter 9:—
> "The infallible Church guarantees the infallibility of the Bible; and the infallible Bible guarantees the infallibility of the Church. But if the Hindu who rested the earth-bearing elephant upon a tortoise, and was met by the question, 'On what then does the tortoise rest?' had answered, 'On the elephant,' the reply would not have very much assisted the querist."

But this writer's "earth-bearing elephant" rests upon a tortoise which rests upon nothing. He claims belief of the facts recorded in the Gospels, but refuses to guarantee that the Gospels are free from error; and when we demand why we should believe them, the answer we get is, "To these facts, in the Church's name, we claim assent." We are to accept the facts, he tells us, not only without raising the question whether the Scriptures which record them are inspired, but without exacting an assurance even that they are true. [1]

> 1] Bishop Gore's creed on this subject is formulated in *Lux Mundi* (see p. 340 especially), a work to which in his more recent treatise on the Church he expressly refers his read-

ers. I have more fully discussed the question in The Buddha of Christendom.

I cite these witnesses merely to confirm what every intelligent thinker must recognize, that faith—or, in other words, Christianity—must have some fixed and sure foundation. And this we have first and chiefly in the words of the Lord Jesus Christ Himself. "Heaven and earth shall pass away," He declared, "but My words shall not pass away." His words were not " inspired": they were absolutely Divine: it is the record of them that is inspired. Nor let anyone object that here my argument moves in a vicious circle. For these pages are addressed to Christians, and the faith of the Christian can have no other basis than the Gospels, regarded as God-breathed Scripture. If I were writing for skeptic s—if the question at issue were the truth of Christianity— my argument would run on different lines.

And from this standpoint it is that we proceed to consider the character of the Bible as a whole. As we have seen, the Hebrew Scriptures are accredited to us by the Lord Himself. His language respecting them is clear and explicit: "The Scriptures cannot be broken." "They are they which testify of Me." "It is easier for heaven and earth to pass, than one tittle of the law to fail." And the resurrection brought no change in His teaching. Kenosis theories, therefore, will avail nothing here. "Beginning at Moses and all the prophets, He expounded unto them in all the Scriptures the things concerning Himself." "And He said unto them, These are the words which I spake unto you while I was yet with you, that all things must be fulfilled which were written in the Law of Moses, and in the Prophets, and in the Psalms, concerning Me." [1] This was the well - known threefold division of the Hebrew Bible —the Law, the Prophets, and the other writings. The Book of Psalms came first in the last division of the Canon, and thus gave its name to the whole. The Bible which the Lord thus unfolded to His disciples was identical with the Old Testament we have in our hands today, not one book or chapter less or more, and He thus accredited it as a whole and in every part as being a testimony to Himself.

1] Luke 24:27, 44.

But the question remains whether the New Testament has equal claims upon our faith.

Chapter 13

Now, first, let us mark the Lord's assurances and promises to those whom He left as His witnesses upon earth. In view of persecution to come, He said this to them, "When they deliver you up, take no thought how or what ye shall speak; for it shall be given you in that same hour what ye shall speak. For it is not ye that speak, but the Spirit of your Father which speaketh in you." [1] At another time, and in a different connection, He said again, "When they bring you before the synagogues, and the rulers, and the authorities, be not anxious how or what ye shall answer, or what ye shall say; for the Holy Spirit shall teach you in that very hour what ye ought to say." [2]

> 1] Matt. 10:19, 20.
>
> 2] Luke 12:11, 12 (R.V.).

If "verbal inspiration" is not here implied, will someone tell us how it could be more clearly described or expressed? Or are we to suppose that these men were to utter Divinely given words when defending themselves before the courts, but that they were to sink to some lower level of inspiration when declaring or expounding truth for the guidance of the Church in all ages? "He that heareth you heareth Me," He said in appointing them to their ministry; [1] and so fully was their testimony to rank with His own, that a worse doom than that of Sodom and Gomorrah shall befall the house or city that refused to "hear their words." [2]

> 1] The fact that these words have been prostituted by the Church of Rome to cover the gigantic imposture of its claims, must not be allowed to rob us of their true meaning and legitimate application.
>
> 4 Matt.10:14, 15.

At the first great Pentecost, we read, "They were all filled with the Holy Ghost and began to speak with other tongues, as the Spirit gave them utterance." Again I ask, if this be not "verbal inspiration," what is? But though thus inspired to preach to a Jerusalem crowd, these same men were left to "sanctified mother wit" when they sat down to write the Gospels which were to be the basis of His people's faith to the end of time!

Here was His promise to them: "The Comforter, the Holy Ghost, whom the Father will send in My name, He shall teach you all things, and bring all things to your remembrance, whatsoever I have said unto you." [1] If these words were fulfilled, there is an end of the inspiration controversy so far as the New Testament is concerned.

1] John 14:26.

Some writers on Inspiration convey the impression that they regard it as a sort of spiritual electricity or steam, which was not to be wasted by supplying more than absolutely necessary. And judging God by their own mean thoughts, they suppose the supply was so stingy as actually to fail of its purpose altogether. For that purpose was not to please or satisfy cranks or critics, but to reveal to us with absolute definiteness and certainty the truth of God for faith to rest upon, and the will of God for heart and life to follow and obey. And any inspiration which comes short of this is practically worthless.

Now when we come to the Epistles we must read them in the light of these promises of inspiration and infallible guidance to those who wrote them. We know the estimate in which, under the Lord's teaching, the Apostle Peter held the Old Testament prophets; and yet he makes those prophets subordinate to the apostles. "Unto whom it was revealed," he writes, "that not unto themselves, but unto us did they minister the things which are now reported unto you by them that have preached the Gospel unto you with the Holy Ghost sent down from heaven." [1] For they had the presence of the Holy Spirit in a new and peculiar sense, unknown even to the prophets of Jehovah. And therefore their words were Divine. "The mouth of Jehovah hath spoken it," was Isaiah's language respecting the great prophecy of comfort, and he added, "the word of our God shall stand forever." And these identical words are applied by the apostle to the apostolic preaching. Their word was "the Word of God" by which believing souls were born again to God—that word which "endureth forever." [2]

> 1] 1 Pet. 1:12. This is to be understood by reference to the Lord's promise that they would have the presence of the Holy Spirit in a special sense different from that in which He was with the people of God before the ascension (John 14:17; 15:26; 16:7, 13).
>
> 2] 1 Pet 1:23-25; Isa. 40:5-8.

If this was not verbal inspiration, what is? But are we to suppose that this enlightenment was limited to Gospel sermons, and denied them when they entered upon the discharge of their highest apostolic functions? [1]

> 1] The Church of Christendom regards the preaching the Gospel to the world as essentially an apostolic function. But this was precisely the ministry which, after Pentecost, the apostles left to the body of believers (Acts 8:1, 4. Mark the words, "except the apostles.").

And not only does the Apostle Peter place apostolic words on a par with those of the greatest of the Hebrew prophets; he goes further and brackets the Epistles of the Apostle Paul with "the other Scriptures" [1]—those holy writings which "cannot be broken," which were held to be "the Word of God"— "the oracles of God."

> 1] 2 Pet. 3:15, 16.

And the Apostle Paul himself, when his authority was questioned in Corinth, wrote such words as these: "If any man think himself to be a prophet, or spiritual, let him acknowledge that the things which I write unto you are the commandments of the Lord." [1]

> 1] Cor. 14:37.

Now in these pages I am not laying down the law, or defending any theory of inspiration. I am writing merely as a Christian to Christians, and dealing with Scripture as I find it. And I have done so in an unconventional way which will shock some old-fashioned people. At the risk of still further offending them, I will ask this question: "If this is not the language of an inspired apostle, and intended to place his Epistle on a par with the very words of His Lord and Master, must we not write him down as either an hysterical fool or an arrogant and profane ecclesiastic?"

And now I ask for special attention to this Apostle's language in the earlier part of this same Epistle: it is the nearest thing the Bible gives to an explanation of inspiration. "Now," he writes, "we have received, not the spirit of the world, but the spirit which is of God; that we might know the things that are freely given us by God. Which things also we speak, not in the words which man's wisdom teacheth, but which the Holy Ghost teacheth, comparing spiritual things with spiritual." [1] For the translation of these last words, the Revisers suggest two alternatives. [2] But to avoid side issues, let us take the passage as it stands. And I ask, If the apostle had in view the suggestion that inspiration extended only to the "things" he wrote, and not to the words in which he wrote them, could he have met it more definitely?

> 1] 1 Cor. 2:12, 13.
>
> 2] The one is to read combining for "comparing," in which case the clause means, "combining the things of the Spirit with the words which the Spirit teaches us to use in regard to them "; and the other is, "interpreting spiritual things to spiritual men."

Not only were his communications about things Divinely revealed, but they were made, not in words such as human wisdom would suggest, but in words taught him by the Spirit of God. Will someone tell us how "verbal inspiration" could be expressed, if this does not express it? Or does the critic again try to escape by the quibble that this kind of inspiration applied only to apostolic speaking, and not to apostolic writing?

Not, I repeat, that such inspiration places the Apostle in the position of the *Planchette* in a spiritualistic séance—as a sort of animated typewriting machine. In inspiration God uses the mind as well as the hand of man, and He gives His revelation in human words—the language of the agent whom He thus employs.

I have dealt thus briefly with the Epistles. Of the Apocalypse I need not speak at all; for all must recognize that if it be not what it claims to be—a Divine revelation—its visions may be dismissed as the lucubration of a disordered brain. And between these alternatives the Christian will not hesitate. It fitly closes the sacred volume. "It recapitulates and confirms all the preceding testimony of prophets and apostles. As it refers to the history of God's kingdom on earth from the Garden of Eden to the reign of David—so it brings before us, in new combinations, and with a light fuller and brighter, the symbolism of Isaiah and Daniel, of Ezekiel and Zechariah. The glorious facts and doctrines revealed in the Gospels and Epistles, are presented here in the most condensed form. Only in the light of its predecessors can this Book be understood. The wonderful and manifold threads laid during many centuries are here connected; the voices of all previous witnesses are blended together for the last time, in harmony majestic and melodious." [1]

1] The words are Adolph Saphir's.

"But," it will be said, "if we come down to the prosaic level of fact, all this is met and answered by the errors of the New Testament; and it is chiefly in the Gospels—the pivot on which all the rest is made to turn, that these errors will be found." This claims consideration, and the following chapters shall be devoted to it.

Chapter 14

To poison a healthy body with the virus of a foul disease is horrible, but yet when smallpox is raging vaccination becomes a duty. And in these days when an epidemic of skepticism prevails, and no one can hear a sermon or read a book without risk of infection, inoculation by a friendly hand may possibly serve to avert a malignant attack of the disease.

Let us be done with grandmotherly theology. The dark ages are past and gone. We belong to an age of enlightenment, The Twentieth Century has dawned. No Protestant, moreover, should fear free thought. To fall back upon authority and traditional beliefs is sheer apostasy from the principles of the Reformation.

Beneath appeals like these there lies a definite element of truth. And, truth or no truth, they are always popular. I am bound, moreover, in honesty to confess that personally I am predisposed to respond to them. Every book I have written gives proof of fearlessness in bringing critical methods to bear upon the study of Scripture. I cannot associate myself with any general campaign against criticism. My quarrel with the Higher Criticism is not because it is criticism, but because, instead of being what it claims to be, it is criticism of a spurious type.

I have already referred to the Ptolemaic System. "Ptolemy the Astronomer was a 'Higher Critic' The belief had long prevailed that the sun was the center of our system ; but he had no difficulty in proving that this traditional belief was untenable. Once he got men to consider the matter from their own standpoint, all could see the absurdity of supposing that the earth on which they lived and moved was flying helter-skelter round the sun. And nothing more was needed but to keep the mind occupied with the many apparent difficulties of the hypothesis he opposed, to the exclusion of all thought of the few but insurmountable difficulties of the theory he advocated. The

Professors and experts were convinced, the multitude followed suit, and for more than a thousand years the puerilities of the Ptolemaic System held sway, with the sanction of infallible science and the blessing of an infallible Church." [1]

    1] *Daniel in the Critics' Den*, 1902 Ed., p. 146.

Let us then turn to study the Scriptures on the "Ptolemaic System." This kind of work is not to my liking, but I think I could do it as well as the Professors. Shutting out God, let us insist on dealing with the Bible from the purely human standpoint, and treat it as a purely human book. Were I writing a many-volumed work, I should like to go over the whole of the Old and New Testament in this way. But here I must be content to take a test case, as the lawyers would say; and I cannot do better than keep to the Gospels. And still further to limit the subject, I will confine myself to the First and the Fourth. I want to inoculate the reader with the skepticism virus.

Apart from superstition and the bondage of received opinions, can any honest-minded person fail to recognize that these Gospels receive their color and mold from the idiosyncrasies of the men who wrote them? Could we not name a "Matthew" and a "John" within the circle of our own acquaintance? Matthew is a man of narrow mind and heart, who has not a thought beyond the interests of his little land and people. The very first sentence of his book gives proof of this. His Messiah is the son of Abraham the Arab chief, and of David the petty tribal king. The triviality of Joseph's pedigree is his next concern. He then goes on to record the birth of the sacred child as connected with a dream and a prophecy; and he makes occasion to bring in a story of his being hailed, even in infancy, as "King of the Jews," and being regarded by king Herod as a rival claimant to his throne.

The preaching attributed to the Messiah is another indication of the writer's character. We all know the sort of man who delights in the pedantry of discarding familiar expressions, and of using phrases peculiar to himself. Such a man was Matthew. Three-and-thirty times he insists on writing "kingdom of heaven," though not one of all the other writers of the New Testament employs the expression even once. It was not that he coined it. He borrowed it from the Book of Daniel, which relates so specially to the fortunes of the Jewish nation.

Then comes "the Sermon on the Mount," that crux of the orthodox. People of a certain sort pretend that the world could be governed on the principles there enunciated; but they are careful not to act on them when their own interests are involved. This is followed by the record of a few extraordinary miracles; and next we come to the sending out of the disciples. And what a commission they received, if Matthew may be trusted! "Go not into the way of the Gentiles, and into any city of the Samaritans enter ye not: but go rather to the lost sheep of the House of Israel." [1] Jews, and none but Jews, are even to hear about the Savior of the world! Could the wit of man frame words more inconsistent with what the rest of the New Testament declares to be the spirit and scope of Christianity! [2]

> 1] Matt. 10:5, 6.
>
> 2] "If Christianity consist of the doctrines preached in the Fourth Gospel it is not too much to say that the Synoptists do not teach Christianity at all. The extraordinary phenomenon is presented of three Gospels, each professing to be complete in itself, and to convey the good tidings of salvation to man, which have actually omitted the doctrines which are the conditions of that salvation" (*Supernatural Religion*, ii. 465).

But why go on? From the first chapter to the last we shall search in vain for a single sentence to raise the narrative above the plane of Jewish interests and hopes. Even the great prophecy recorded in the twenty-fourth chapter has Jerusalem for its center. And the vision of judgment in the chapter which follows represents blessing or doom to the Gentiles according as they befriended or persecuted the favored nation. And finally, even the great commission after the resurrection is represented here as addressed to Jews, charging them to baptize and teach the Gentiles. [1]

> 1] This is true; but the inference here drawn from it is, I need not say, entirely false. The commission is a prophetic one. See *The Buddha of Christendom*, pp. 270-273.

The change from the First Gospel to the Fourth is like emerging from a gloomy cloister to the free air of heaven and the open sunshine. The True Light was in the world—His own world, the world that He had made. "The Word was made flesh and dwelt among us, full of grace and truth." And the secret of His coming was because God loved the world; and the purpose of it was "that whosoever believeth in Him should not perish, but have eternal life." Whosoever. The narrow channel of a nation's hopes is lost in the great wide sea of Divine love. And there is life, and not judgment, for the sinner who believes. "For God sent not His Son into the world to condemn the world; but that the world through Him might be saved."

But here a doubt obtrudes itself: a cloud appears and shuts out our sunshine. If the peculiarities of the First Gospel be due to the character of the writer of it, may not also the distinctive features of the Fourth be thus accounted for. And if it be clear that both cannot be inspired, what ground is left for claiming a Divine authorship for either?

Difficulties and doubts of this kind troubled me even before I left school. But fortunately I did not then know that they were supposed to be proof of abnormal cleverness. For though in childhood I often met a pundit who, as I afterwards discovered, was one of the pioneers of Higher Criticism in this country, he never tried to corrupt the faith of the young, as so many of his successors do today. And had he done so he might possibly have failed to influence me; for we children were impressed not so much by his great learning as by his great silliness. So in my schoolboy days, instead of thinking I was very clever, I took for granted I was very wicked; and I generally dismissed the matter in the hope that when I became a Christian in the true and real sense, I should be able to read the Bible differently, and to understand things which then seemed to me inexplicable—a hope that was in due time realized, though not in the transcendental way that I expected.

Some people seem to enjoy parading their inner experiences. To me it is an ordeal. But I will submit to it if others can be helped thereby. In the first enthusiasm of my Christian life I gave no thought to difficulties such as these. But there are times, as every Christian knows, "when neither sun nor stars in many days appear, and no small tempest lies on us"; and at a crisis of this kind these difficulties all came back; and in the light of knowledge gained in my college days, they seemed more utterly insoluble than ever.

Men place in parallel columns the events recorded in the Evangelists' narratives, and call this a "Harmony of the Gospels." What I wanted was a clue to some sort of harmony in the doctrines they taught. A systematic study of them brought me no relief. I could make something of the Synoptists, as they are called; but John refused to blend with Matthew. I turned to Commentaries and " Introductions," and found in them almost everything except what I was in search of. If I could have satisfied myself that the Fourth Gospel was Divinely inspired, I should have been willing to throw over the other three. But proof of this was wanting. It was written long after the other Gospels, and therefore, viewed as a human document, it was less trustworthy than the rest.

Discoveries of this kind delight a Higher Critic; to me they gave only pain. If a man has cogent proof that his father is a rogue or his wife unfaithful, he must face the fact, and consider how to act on it . But one who would accept the proof with alacrity and pleasure is not more utterly contemptible than the man who can contemplate the collapse of faith in the Bible without distress, if not dismay. I kept my difficulties to myself, until a lecture I heard one evening in a friend's drawing-room gave me a clue to the solution of them; and the Bible became a new book to me from that hour. At this point I will drop the personal element in my narrative, and give in another chapter the results attained. To describe the steps by which those results were reached would be, if not uninteresting, at least unprofitable.

Chapter 15

"The Bible is the history of man." "The Gospels were written to teach the way of salvation." These are but specimens of popular errors which serve to make those who hold them an easy prey to the skeptic s.

Save for a brief preface of eleven chapters, covering a period measured by thousands of years, the burden of the Old Testament is the story of the Hebrew race. And the first book of the New Testament is the sequel and conclusion of the Old. The Gospels are not a set of faulty and erring narratives, written with a common object. Their purpose in the Divine scheme of revelation is to present the Lord Jesus Christ in the four great aspects of His mission and work, [1] as Israel's Messiah, Jehovah's Servant, Son of Man and Son of God. And it is by a true instinct that earnest souls turn to the Fourth Gospel when they seek the path of life; for the words which close the twentieth chapter describe the contents of every page, "These are written that ye might believe that Jesus is the Christ, the Son of God; and that believing ye might have life through His name."

> 1] "Four discriminated aspects of their common subject, . . . but one portrait" (Bampton Lectures, 1864).

I must adhere to the limits I have set myself, and deal only here with Matthew and John. Does any Christian really believe that the striking differences between the two, from first to last, can be explained on the theory that the one apostle was a bigoted Jew and the other a dreamy enthusiast?

And if the Gospels be mere human documents, nothing less than this will account for the facts. Both men received the same teaching throughout the whole period of the Ministry. Both heard those "most sacred of all sacred words" uttered upon the eve of the Crucifixion. Both were re-commissioned in the same terms after the resurrection.

And yet as we study the First Gospel—I here repeat as fact and truth what I have already suggested as a skeptical difficulty — "From the first chapter to the last we shall search in vain for a single sentence to raise the narrative above the plane of Jewish interests and hopes."

Let me give a startling instance of the contrast in the teaching. The Fourth Gospel tells of eternal life as the free gift of God to every sinner who believes in Christ; whereas in the First Gospel the only passages where eternal life is mentioned, [1] deal with it on strictly Old Testament lines. There are two possible explanations of all this. Either one of the apostles of the Lord—men specially chosen to be His witnesses in a wholly peculiar sense — deliberately set himself to misrepresent his Master's mission and pervert His teaching; or else he did this innocently, through sheer stupidity and ignorance. Will any Christian dare to identify himself with either of these hypotheses? Can anyone —Christian or not — suggest a third?

> 1] Matt. 19:16, 29; 25:40-46.

Yes, a third is possible; but it assumes that the Gospels are not mere human records. "Christ was a minister of the circumcision for the truth of God to confirm the promises made unto the fathers." [1] And "the Hebrew Gospel," as it is sometimes called, is the Divine record of this "Ministry of the Circumcision."

> 1] Rom. 15:8. The next verse runs on, "And that the Gentiles might glorify God for His mercy." To the people of the covenant His coming was a matter of promise: to Gentiles (who are "strangers from the covenants of promise" — Ephes. 2:12), it was pure mercy. The Divine accuracy of Holy Scripture never misses distinctions such as this.

With this clue to guide us we shall find that the very same characteristics which, in my case at least, tempted to unbelief, now establish faith. People read the New Testament backwards, and with erroneous preconceptions of its scheme and scope; and when they reach its preface they demand, "What has a Jewish genealogy to do with the advent of the Son of God as the Savior of the world?" The answer is, "Absolutely nothing"; and the Gospel which so presents Him omits even the mention of His birth. The Bible opens with the declaration, "In the beginning created God" [1] so here, "In the beginning was The Word. [2] And then, "The Word was made flesh and dwelt among us." How made flesh it matters not. "He was in the world, and the world was made by Him, and the world knew Him not. But as many as received Him to them gave He the right to become children of God, even to them that believe on His name."

> 1] Gen. 1:1. This is the order of the words in the Hebrew.
>
> 2] John 1:1.

The casual reader will miss nothing from these words; and yet the omission I have made is one of the utmost moment. I have quoted the tenth and twelfth verses; here is the eleventh: "He came unto His own, and His own received Him not." [1]

> 1 Our English idiom cannot express the meaning here: the margin of R.V. gives one of the "schoolboy translations" that so often mar that work. The French is more apt: "Il est venu chez soi, et les siens ne l'ont point recu."

This brief sentence gives the whole purpose and scope of the First Gospel. Now we can appreciate its opening words, "The book of the generation of Jesus Christ, the son of David, the son of Abraham." He was "a minister of the circumcision," the earthly people of the covenant — "of whom," as the Apostle Paul declares, "is Christ as concerning the flesh." [1] And he speaks of Him again as "of the seed of David." [2] Hence His genealogy is traced to Abraham, the father of the covenant and the founder of the race, and to David, the head of the royal house. [3] Hence, too, the emphasis laid upon the fact of his birth in Bethlehem, the royal city.

> 1] Rom. 9:5, R.V.
>
> 2] 2 Tim. 2:8.
>
> 3] As regards the difference between the genealogies of Matthew and Luke, see Appendix, Note IV.

Let me repeat all this in borrowed words. "The record of St. Matthew, ever recognized as the Hebrew Gospel, is the true commencement of the New Testament, showing how it grows out of the Old, and presenting the manifestation of the Son of God not as a detached phenomenon, but as the predestined completion of the long course of historic dispensations. It is the Book of the generation of Jesus Christ, the Son of David, the Son of Abraham. It founds itself on the ideas of the old covenant. It refers at every step, especially in its earlier chapters, to the former Scriptures, noting how that was fulfilled which was spoken by the prophets. It is a history of fulfilment, presenting the Lord as the fulfiller of all righteousness, the fulfiller of the Law and the Prophets, not come to destroy, but to fulfil. It sets Him forth as a King and Lawgiver in that kingdom of heaven for which a birthplace and a home had been prepared in Israel: and thus corresponds to that period in the historical course of events when the word was preached to none but to the Jews only." [1]

> 1] Canon Bernard's *Progress of Doctrine in the New Testament*, being the "Bampton Lectures," 1864. This book, long out of print, but now happily reissued, is one of the most valuable of the Bampton series. Such another, though of a wholly different character, is Dr. Hatch's volume of 1880. Though *The Organization of the Early Christian Churches* is one of the greatest theological books of the age, it appears to be systematically "boycotted" by High Church and Low Church alike.

And now it only remains for me to give, in this new light, a brief sketch of the contents of Matthew's Gospel. The briefest will suffice; for others will find, as I did, that once the key is in their hands, they can open the treasure for themselves. One proviso, however, is essential. The Old Testament teems with prophecies and promises relating to the Jewish race. But the way some people dispose of these is to appropriate most of them to the Gentile Church of this dispensation, and to dismiss the rest as Hebrew poetry. And with this sort of "interpretation" of Scripture I can make no terms. Those who adopt it may skip the rest of this chapter: it will have no meaning for them.

Between the second chapter of Matthew and the third, there is an interval of more than thirty years. The third chapter speaks of the Baptist's mission, and records the baptism of Christ. The Old Testament closes with the promise, " Behold, I will send you Elijah the prophet"; and the opening page of the New Testament tells of the ministry of him who came "in the spirit and power of Elias." John was Elijah, if they would receive him. [1] The baptism of Christ is an enigma to those who attach a pagan meaning to the ordinance. His purpose was to identify Himself with the true remnant of the nation. Then followed "the Temptation"; and "from that time" His ministry began. The Lord Himself took up the Baptist's testimony, "Repent, for the kingdom of heaven is at hand." [2] Literally, "the kingdom of the heavens"—an expression used three and thirty times in Matthew, and never once again in the New Testament. [3] The fulfilment was at hand of all that God had prophesied and promised of a time when the heavens would rule over the earth — a reign of righteousness and peace.

> 1] Matt. 11:14, R.V. (margin). On this passage see by all means Dean Alford's note, as a correction to the prevailing skepticism on this subject.
>
> 2] See Matt. 3:2; 4:17; 10:7.
>
> 3] See Appendix, Note V.

The closing verses of the fourth chapter receive but little notice, and yet their importance in the narrative is immense. "He went about All Galilee teaching in their synagogues and preaching the gospel of the kingdom and healing All manner of sickness and All manner of disease among the people. And His fame went throughout all Syria; and they brought unto Him All sick people . . . and He healed them. And there followed Him great multitudes of people" from every part of all the land.

The seeming triumph of this first circuit of the Ministry led to the proclamation of the principles of that kingdom which He preached—the spiritual and moral atmosphere which must prevail where God rules. For such is the purpose of the Sermon on the Mount. Men are always ready for Divine blessing if only they can have it on their own terms. If after working such miracles the Lord had proclaimed a holy war, the nation would have rallied round Him. Or had He proclaimed His "brotherhood " with fallen man — had He preached a "gospel of humanity" — their heathen conquerors even might have hailed Him as a deliverer and carried Him in triumph to the deserted palace of the Caesars; for never, perhaps, before or since, was the pagan world so full of weariness and despair as in the hateful reign of Tiberius. M [1]

> 1] During the period of the Ministry, Tiberius was absent from Rome. He had withdrawn to the island of Capreae, where he gave himself up to an orgy of sensuality.

But His purpose was far different. Christendom has taught, throughout its history, that by His advent He fulfilled the law and ignored the prophets; His contemporaries looked to Him to fulfil the prophets while accepting their own interpretation of the law. But the Sermon on the Mount makes it as clear as light that if the heavens are to rule the earth, the will of God must be "done on earth as it is done in heaven." [1]

> 1] That the question should even be raised whether the Sermon on the Mount should guide men now in government is proof of the hopeless ignorance of Scripture which prevails. It is teaching for the governed in the days of the kingdom. Its principles are eternal, but some of the definite precepts of this "kingdom" teaching were expressly cancelled by our Lord Himself (see, e.g., Luke 22:35, 36). The common belief appears to be that the Lord's presence or absence is an element of no importance whatever. But that is not His view of the matter!

The narrative next records a series of miracles of special significance. There was One in Israel who could put His hand upon a leper and yet be undefiled [1]; who could heal the sick by a word, [2] or by a touch [3]; who could command the winds and waves, [4] and control the powers of hell [5]; who could not only heal the body, but cure and save the soul.[6] And as a crowning public proof that His power reached to the under world, He could even raise the dead. [7]

> 1] Matt.8:3.
> 2] Ibid. 8:13.
> 3] Ibid. 8:15.
> 4] Ibid. 8:26.
> 5] Ibid. 8:28-32.
> 6] Ibid. 9:2.
> 7] Ibid. 9:25.

This was the period of His personal ministry. He afterwards commissioned the Apostles, giving them the same powers He Himself had exercised, [1] and entrusting them with the same testimony, "The kingdom of heaven is at hand." Hence the limit placed upon their ministry; for "the kingdom of heaven" is the Messianic kingdom in its earthly aspect.

> 1] Ibid. 10:8.

Chapter 12 records the crisis which changed the entire character of His public ministry. The religious leaders of the nation had seen His miracles and heard His words—they had received all the public proofs of His Messiahship; and what was their response? They "went out and took counsel against Him how they might destroy Him." [1] The Lord's answer was to "withdraw Himself;" and though the multitudes which crowded after Him still proved His power to heal, instead of bidding them, as in the past, to tell others of His fame, He "charged them that they should not make Him known." The chapter closes with words of awful judgment upon that "wicked generation" "that had thus rejected Him. [2]

1] Matt 12:14.

2] Ver. 45.

His rejection gave a new character also to His teaching. Till then it had been open: now it became veiled in parables. The rejection of the light brings judicial blindness. The parables were given that all might hear the new phase of "kingdom" teaching, but that only those whose eyes and ears were spiritually open should know and understand it. [1]

1] Matt. 13:10-17.

No greater contribution has ever been made to theology than will be his who fully and intelligently elucidates the teaching of the thirteenth chapter of Matthew. It contains seven parables. The first is the preface to the rest, and governs them all. The Divine description of their subject and scope is "the mysteries of the kingdom of heaven." [1] There was nothing secret about the kingdom foretold in prophecy and preached by the Lord and His apostles. But a heavenly kingdom in which a king reigning in righteousness gives place to a sower sowing seed, is an utter enigma. The theories of expositors here are no answer to the ridicule of rationalists. But the Divine explanation of the "mystery" silences both the ridicule and the theories.

1] Ver. 11.

Human apostasy and sin cannot thwart God's purposes, but they may and do postpone the fulfilment of them. The disciples themselves came to understand that, on account of their Lord's rejection, there was to be another "coming." [1] These parables give us the key to the whole intervening period. The first unfolds the "mystery" of an unseen Sower taking the place of a manifested ruler. The next three describe the public effects of the ministry of "the Sower." These, together with the prefatory parable, were spoken to the multitude: the final three, together with the interpretation of the parable of the tares were spoken privately to the disciples, [2] and they teach what is essential and secret.

1] Matt. 24:3.

1] Matt. 13:36.

In the earlier phase of the Ministry "signs" were openly given, abundantly sufficient to satisfy the doubts and silence the cavils of the Pharisees. [1] But when, after they had thus proved themselves to be "a wicked and adulterous generation," they again sought a "sign," the answer they received was a definite refusal. The only miracle they were to witness now was that of the Prophet Jonah—the death and resurrection of their rejected Messiah. [2] And following upon this, He forbade all further testimony to His Messiahship. In this later phase of His ministry He had enjoined silence upon those who benefited by His "signs"; now He forbade even His disciples to tell anyone that He was the Christ, and He unfolded to them the mystery of His Passion. [3]

1] See, e.g., John 2:23; 3:2, R.V.

2] Matt. 16:1-4.

3] Ibid. 16:20, 21, R.V.

But exigencies of space forbid my pursuing the subject further in detail. As regards the great prophecy of the twenty-fourth chapter, I will only say here that it deals, not with "the end of the world," but with the consummation of the age [1] — the events which are to mark the close of "the evil age which has set in." [2]

1] Matt. 24:3 (R.V. margin). The word used in verse 3 is sunteleia (cf. Heb. 9:26); the word telos is employed in verse 6. Matt. 24 has been well described by Dean Alford as "the anchor of apocalyptic interpretation." I have dealt with it in chapter xiii. of The Coming Prince.

2] Gal. 1:4. The "age" here intended is that of chapter 13, which is to end with the return of Christ to establish His kingdom. And then "the mystery of God will be finished" — the mystery that a God of infinite power and goodness permits evil to prevail in the world (Rev. 10:7; 11:15). That will not be an "evil age," and God's people will not need deliverance from it. "The evil age which has set in" is the age during which Christ is rejected.

In conclusion let me restate this part of my argument. If we are to regard Matthew as a merely human book, we find ourselves compelled to account for its peculiar characteristics in either of two ways. Either the writer, albeit he was an apostle of the Lord, and shared all His teaching, remained in utter ignorance of the distinctive truths of Christianity; or else, with a knowledge of these truths, he perversely and wickedly concealed or distorted them.

The critic must make choice between these alternatives. But the Christian refuses both; for he rejects the assumption on which both are based.

To him the First Gospel is not a mere human treatise, but a Divine revelation; and grasping the thought that the purpose of that revelation was to present Christ as Israel's Messiah, he accounts for the extraordinary phenomena of the book in the only way in which they can be reasonably explained, namely, that the Spirit of God so guided and restrained both the mind and the hand of the writer, that his narrative from first to last does not contain a single sentence inconsistent with the Divine purpose with which it was written.

It is not that the Lord's words were not accurately recorded by the Evangelists, but that, while His teaching covered the whole field of truth, the inspiring Spirit led the writers to discriminate, so that each gave prominence to that aspect of it which he was used to present. A commander-in-chief may lay before his generals his whole plan of battle, but when he issues his orders each brigadier receives only what it concerns him to know. The infantry are not told what part the cavalry will have to play, and neither is informed where the artillery will be placed. So was it with the Lord and His teaching. In the very same discourses probably He unfolded to the apostles the truth relating to the kingdom of heaven, and kindred truth in relation to the wider sphere of the kingdom of God. [1] But though these men heard the same words, and though no doubt they discussed them together times without number, the fact remains that when they came to write, these various aspects of truth were kept distinct. If this is to be explained on natural principles, it is a phenomenon which is absolutely without parallel in human experience.

    1] See Appendix, Note V.

Chapter 16

These skeptical critics always remind me of the amateur detective. The amateur detective is strong on details. But he generally enters upon an inquiry with a fixed preconception as to what he is going to find, and he exhausts his power of attention upon trifles that seem to point in the direction on which his mind is set. The trained expert, on the other hand, coming in with an open mind and a wider knowledge, will seize on clues that the amateur has missed.

The microscope serves to make the wonders of nature seem all the more wonderful, and no criticism of Scripture can be too searching and minute, if only it be intelligent and spiritual. Such criticism, moreover, is an antidote to the criticism of the skeptic s. For if "knowledge is power," ignorance is weakness. And in no sphere is this more true than in the spiritual. But the knowledge that is wanting is the knowledge of Holy Scripture. For All Scripture is profitable, that the man of God may be "ready at every point." [1] And we cannot with impunity neglect large sections of Scripture which are inextricably interwoven with the rest.

1] 2 Tim. 3:17. Thus it is that Alford renders it.

The doctrine of the "Second Advent," as theologians call it, will serve as a notable illustration of this. The New Testament speaks of the coming of the Son of Man to earth, to bless His people upon earth. It speaks of the descent of the Lord from heaven, and of His people being caught up from earth to meet Him. It speaks of His coming as a bridegroom to claim a bride. It speaks of His coming as a king to receive a kingdom. It speaks of His feet standing on the Mount of Olives, "in like manner" as He stood there with His disciples on the day of His ascension. It speaks of His being revealed from heaven with His mighty angels in flaming fire, taking vengeance. It speaks of the dead, small and great, being arraigned before the great white throne above. It speaks of the living nations upon earth being gathered before His judgment throne of glory.

Now what are we to make of all these conflicting statements? A dull Evangelicalism in the past was content to read them at different times, and to believe them all without attempting to understand them. But to maintain such an attitude in the face of modern criticism is to court disaster as certainly as if we were to face modern artillery with the ordnance used at Waterloo. Scripture itself must teach us how all these apparently irreconcilable statements can be reconciled.

But first let us hear what the critics have to say about them. We turn for enlightenment to the standard work already quoted, Dr. Hastings's *Dictionary of the Bible*, of which Professor Driver of Oxford is one of the principal editors. The article entitled "Parousia" [1] deals with this subject. Its effort to harmonise the passages fails. They represent, we are told, "two distinct types of thought." In the one "the Parousia is conceived after the analogy of the contemporary Jewish Apocalypses": in the other "the Parousia is rather the completion of an order of things already existing." "The question naturally presents itself as to which of these two types most fairly represents the teaching of our Lord." If to this question a clear answer can be given, all will be well. But the general result is that the confusion is due to "an imperfect apprehension by the disciples of the Master's meaning." [2]

> 1] A Greek word meaning "the coming," or (as, e.g., in 2 Cor. 10:10 and Phil. 2:12) "the presence."

> 2] The alternative, we are told, would be "to believe that He, who in all other respects possessed an insight so much clearer than His contemporaries, should, in the matter of eschatology alone, *have had nothing new to contribute.*" The italics are mine, and they are designed to call attention to the manner in which some men dare to speak of their Divine Lord.

The only certain thing, therefore, is the utter uncertainty that exists as to the truth upon this subject. Not a single statement in the New Testament relating to the future Coming is worthy of confidence. And as the New Testament writers may not be trusted on this most vital issue, no clear-headed, sensible person will give implicit belief to their words respecting any of the transcendental doctrines of

Christianity. Faith is impossible. Agnosticism becomes the only rational attitude of mind.

But this does not solve the difficulty. How, then, are all these conflicting statements to be explained? Now what would be the thought of one who tried to reconcile the prescriptions of some eminent physician, and then denounced him because the effort failed? Such a genius would not be more unintelligent than are these exponents of "the best and latest scholarship." Prescriptions differ because the cases to which they apply are different. And the predictions of the Parousia differ for a like reason.

The Bible teems with prophecies and promises relating to earth, which still await fulfilment. And not one of these shall fail. God has not "cast away His people whom He foreknew." Israel's rejected Messiah is to return; and "they shall look upon Him whom they pierced, and mourn." Meanwhile this Gentile dispensation has intervened; for Israel's temporary loss is our eternal gain. And God has purposes for earth that reach beyond a gathered Church and a restored nation. "The earth shall be full of the knowledge of the Lord": this is not a rhetorical shriek, but a Divine prophecy. "Thy will be done on earth as it is done in heaven" is not a day-dream of pious fools, but an inspired prayer for the realization of a Divine purpose plainly revealed in Scripture. This very earth, so cursed and blighted by human sin, shall yet be the scene of a display of Divine power and goodness, bringing glory to God and blessing to mankind.

Mingling with these manifold displays of grace there will be sessions of judgment. And all are included in "the doctrine of the Parousia." For every purpose of God, whether of judgment or of grace, is headed up in Christ; and therefore in the unfolding of these purposes there will be many manifestations of Christ. And while the Higher Criticism, in keeping with its persistent ignorance of Divine truth, takes all these many Scriptures, and throwing them into "hotch-pot" (as the lawyers would say), parades the resulting mass of confusion and error and folly as the outcome of superior enlightenment, the spiritual Christian will seek humbly and reverently to "sort" each of these Divine prophecies (as Lord Bacon puts it) "with the event fulfilling the same," assigning to each its right place in the grand scheme of revelation. [1]

> 1] There is nothing exceptional about this "Parousia" article. On the contrary, it is a fair specimen of the pompous

> pedantry of book-scholarship, combined with a special type of ignorance characteristic of writers of this school. I use the word "ignorance" deliberately, for while they pose as the apostles of a new enlightenment in the exposition of the New Testament, their writings give proof that, as already urged, they are ignorant of "the word of the beginning of Christ"—the very language in which the book is written.

And that phase of Evangelicalism which shares the ignorance of the critics leaves the Bible an easy prey to their attacks. If the Christian neglects the Bible he cannot be "ready at every point." The "doctrine of the types," for instance, is not an abstruse branch of study which, like a "special subject" in a school curriculum, may safely be ignored. It bears upon the most elementary truths.

Many years ago I was present at a conference convened to consider what people call "the simple Gospel." Among the clergymen who took part in the discussion there were two of considerable note as teachers. Before half an hour elapsed one of them had practically unfurled the banner of Calvinism, and the other that of Arminianism. According to the one, Christ has borne the sins of His people; and though the Gospel is to be preached to all, salvation is only for the elect. According to the other, Christ has borne the sins of the whole world, and the doom of the impenitent will be due to their rejection of the Gospel.

Now both these positions cannot be right, and yet both can appeal to numerous passages of the New Testament which seem to support them. Where then are we to find the key to the enigma? The typology of the Pentateuch is the Divine picture alphabet which God has given to enable us to spell out these truths; and if, whether from carelessness or arrogance, we neglect it, we are sure to fall into error. Calvinism assumes that the sin-offering exhausts the doctrine of the Gospel. But the sin-offering is only one of many kindred types, and all are needed to unfold in its fullness the sacrifice of Christ. True it is that the sin-offering was only for the redeemed people; but it was not by the sin-offering that they obtained redemption. When we speak of Christ's bearing our sins, we use a figurative expression; but the figure is not rhetorical but typical, and the sin-offering is the type which explains it. Therefore it is that Scripture never speaks of Christ's "bearing the sins of the world." He is "the propitiation for the sins of the whole world;" and forgiveness of sins is to be preached to all, for "He gave Himself a ransom for all;" [1] "He came to be "the Savior of the world." [2]

> 1] 1 Tim. 2:6.
>
> 2] 1 John 4:14.

But what of the Baptist's testimony, "Behold the Lamb of God that taketh away the sin of the world"? [1] I do not forget it. But in the accuracy of Scripture language there is a definite difference between "bearing the sins of the world," and "taking away the sin of the world."

> 1] John 1:29.

"What hair-splitting!" someone will here exclaim. Yes; in attacking or perverting Scripture, attention to the minutest and most trivial points is "Higher Criticism"; but in the defense of Scripture it is hyper-criticism! The special truth of the sin-offering is the identification of the offerer with the victim. Substitution is but a half-truth. But there can be no identification with Christ until we receive the Gospel. Then it is, and not till then, that we become one with Him. And if one with Him, His death is our death, and we can adopt the words, "His own self bare our sins in His own body on the tree."

This is the language of the sin-offering. But in the Passover, by which redemption was obtained, there was no laying on of hands, no previous identification of the sinner with the victim. The victim died for the sinner's sins, but it was by the sprinkling of its blood that the sinner obtained the benefit of the sacrifice. The Gospel by which we are saved is that "Christ died for our sins according to the Scriptures," and faith is the counterpart of the sprinkling of the blood. [1]

> 1] Dean Alford explains John 1:29 by reference directly to Isa. 53:7, and presumably to the sin-offering. But the bracketing of the slaughtered lamb with the shorn sheep in the prophecy clearly proves that the words do not refer to the offerings, but present the Messiah as the innocent and uncomplaining victim of the violence of men. Moreover the word there rendered "slaughter" is not a sacrificial term. It is never used of killing for sacrifice; never at all in the Pentateuch, save in Gen. 43:16. And the word trans-

lated "laid on" in verse 6 is never once used in connection with the offerings or sacrifices.

The sin-offering typified Christ's bearing the sins of His people. But redemption involves a larger question than this. For man is not merely a committer-of-sins, but a sinner in a deeper sense. He belongs to a sinful race. I am not discussing the philosophy of skeptical expositors, but the plain teaching of Scripture. "Through one trespass the judgment is unto all men to condemnation." [1] Not that all men shall be in fact condemned, for the believer "shall not come into condemnation"; [2] but this is the scope and tendency of the judgment. And "Even so, through one righteous act, [3] the free gift is unto all men to justification of life." Not that all are justified, but that this is the scope and tendency of the grace. Words could not teach more plainly that the death of Christ is as far-reaching as the sin of Adam. By that death He has taken away the sin of the world, and God has reconciled the world to Himself. [4]

>1] Rom. 5:18.
>
>2] John 5:24.
>
>3] Δικαίωμα— "an amendment of a wrong; hence, judgment, punishment" (Liddell and Scott).
>
>4] 2 Cor. 5:19.

With the critics the types of the Pentateuch are but a part of "the priestly code," which was based on the success or failure (I know not which) of the ministry of the prophets. They have no Divine significance whatever. But with the intelligent Christian these types are "the word of the beginning of Christ." He turns to the New Testament to find the doctrine relating to each one of them, and he turns back to the Pentateuch, as to a key-picture, to make sure that he has overlooked nothing in the doctrinal teaching of Christianity. If, for example, as we have seen, he reads of Christ as a Sin-bearer, he studies the Sin-offering; if he reads of the "lamb" of our redemption, the Passover; if of the blood of the New Covenant by which we are sanctified, and of which the cup of the Lord's Supper is the sign and emblem, then the twenty-fourth chapter of Exodus unfolds its depth of meaning. [1]

>1] See *The Buddha of Christendom*, ch. 12.

Chapter 16   139

These paragraphs are humbly offered as instances of true criticism in contrast with the criticisms of the critics. Such instances might be multiplied indefinitely. And in such proofs of the absolute accuracy and hidden unity of Scripture, the Christian finds overwhelming cumulative evidence of its Divine origin and authority.

Chapter 17

In the course of a summer visit many years ago at one of the historic homes of Ireland, an incident occurred which often comes to my mind as I read the criticisms of the critics upon the Gospel narratives.

The eldest son and daughter of the house left us one morning to spend the day with relatives some half-dozen miles away. Late at night, from my bedroom window, I saw the returning carriage drive up to the hall door. The lady alighted with a gentleman who was not her brother. At breakfast next morning she told us that her brother had remained at his cousin's house, and she had brought back a Mrs. Somebody—mentioning a name I did not know. Owing to the disturbed state of the country, surprise was expressed that two ladies should have thus driven home alone at night. This enabled me to press the question whether a gentleman had not escorted her; and her answer was unequivocal that her only companion had been the lady she named.

When in my official life I have found a conflict of testimony between persons of known integrity, I have always sought some way of reconciling them. But in this case I confess I was baffled; and had I not had more confidence in my friend than the critics have in the Bible, I should have given her up as being utterly untruthful, and perhaps worse. But I afterwards obtained from her the solution of the enigma. The lady she named was the wife of their doctor. His house was near the gate of the park; and when his wife alighted he took her place in the carriage and drove with my friend to the hall door.

Not all the Biblical critics of Christendom can find in Scripture a more hopeless conflict of testimony than would have been my friend's account, and my own, of her return to her father's house that night. If we had both written about it without first comparing notes, I should have asserted that her only companion was a gentleman; she would have declared that her only companion was a lady. "Sherlock Holmes" himself could have made nothing of it. And yet the solution of it seems ludicrously simple when all the facts are known. She was thinking of her six miles' drive; I, of her arrival at the house. Both accounts, therefore, would have been absolutely true, though to all appearance one or other would have seemed absolutely false; and anyone who attempted to play the rôle of "reconciler" would have fared badly at the hands of the critics.

There are difficulties in the Gospel narratives which appear equally inexplicable. And the efforts of zealous "reconcilers" to explain them sometimes do more harm than good. They probably admit of some very simple explanation, which would be obvious if all the circumstances were in view. The question, however, to which they give rise in the mind, I will not say of a competent critic, still less of a spiritual Christian, but of any person endowed with common sense— a quality which seems to be sometimes lacking to both Christians and critics—concerns the general character of the writings thus seemingly impugned. And here I am not assuming that the Evangelists were inspired, but merely that they were competent and trustworthy witnesses.

To introduce into this book a glossary of difficult passages would be wholly foreign to its scope: indeed it would make it unreadable. In the preceding chapters I have selected illustrative examples of the objections dealt with, and I will still pursue the same course. I will proceed to give instances of difficulties which appear insoluble, of others which are easily explained, and of a third class which indicate only the perversity or the ignorance of those who urge them.

Of the class first mentioned I know of no case more apt than that of the blind men outside Jericho. [1] A definite contradiction seems to mark the Gospel narratives. I am not referring to the fact that Matthew mentions two men as healed on the occasion, whereas Mark and Luke speak of one only. The received explanation of this — that "the sources from which each Evangelist took his narrative" differed in this way —is strangely shallow and unintelligent, for this only puts the "difficulty" one step back. But a little knowledge of human nature and of real life will oust that "difficulty" altogether. If either Evangelist said that the Lord cured only one blind man on the occasion, the matter would be different. But one of the two men was evidently a well-known character — "blind Bartimeus" — while the other, possibly, was a stranger to the locality. Two of the Evangelists speak only of the man who was known: Mark names him, and Luke refers to him as "a certain blind man." To represent this as a "contradiction" bespeaks the perversity of fools.

    1] See Matt. 20:29-34 ; Mark 10:46-52; and Luke 18:35-43.

But a very real difficulty remains; Luke represents the incident as occurring when the Lord was approaching Jericho, while the other Gospels say expressly that it was when He was leaving the town. The contradiction here seems as hopeless as that recorded in my Irish story. Possibly, however, the explanation of it would be just as simple; but I, at least, decline to play the role of "Sherlock Holmes" in dealing with Holy Scripture.

A popular preacher and writer who is one of the lesser lights of the Higher Criticism has published the statement that in his Oxford days "the whole foundation" of his faith was shaken by discovering that, in Acts 5:36, Gamaliel is said to have mentioned an insurrection under one Theudas, whereas Josephus records an insurrection under a man of that name half a century later; the inference being, of course, that the Evangelist was thus proved to have blundered.

Who among us has not been equally silly at times! But some of us are shrewd enough to conceal our silliness from other people. There are three possible explanations of the difficulty, any one of which would suffice. First, in any conflict of statement between a writer so accurate as Luke, and a writer so notoriously inaccurate as Josephus, the presumption of error is entirely against the historian, and not against the Evangelist. [1] Secondly, it is very probable that the Theudas of Gamaliel's speech is one of the insurgents mentioned by Josephus under another name. But thirdly, the whole difficulty assumes that the historian enumerates all these insurrections, whereas, in fact, he declares there were "thousands" of them; and one Theudas may well have been the leader of such an outbreak before "the days of the taxing," and another Theudas may have headed a similar revolt during the reign of Claudius. [2]

> 1] For the sake of argument I here treat the Third Gospel as a merely human book.
>
> 2] *Antiquities*, 17:10, 4, and 20:5, 1. Josephus mentions three Judases within ten years, and four Simons within forty years as leaders of such revolts. There may well,

therefore, have been two named Theudas in the same half-century.

Among the difficulties which, though easily explained, seem to unsettle the faith of a certain sort of people, there is one that may serve to illustrate the perverseness of some of the German critics. "Verily I say unto you," the Lord declared in telling of the dread events which are to herald His return, "this generation shall not pass till all these things be fulfilled." [1] What meaning can possibly be given Up to these words, save that the Parousia was to occur in the lifetime of those to whom He spoke? The question is answered by a fact well known to the critics themselves, that the word here rendered *generation* "has in Hellenistic Greek the meaning of a race, or family of people." [2]

1] Matt. 24:34.

2] Alford's Greek Testament; and see any Lexicon.

And any intelligent reader can see that in other passages also it is used in that sense. [1] The Jews, instead of suffering the fate of every other conquered race in all the world's history, were to remain a separate people to the end. The Lord's words, therefore, instead of proving a stumbling-block ought rather to establish our faith.

1] See, e.g., chap, 23:36, and various passages in the LXX., as, e.g., Gen. 31:3 ; Jer. 8:3.

People seem to be strangely troubled about the Inscription upon the Cross. Dean Alford writes :—

> "The title over the cross was written in Greek. According then to the verbal-inspiration theory, each Evangelist has recorded the exact words of the inscription; not the general sense, but the inscription itself —not a letter less or more. This is absolutely necessary to the theory." (Com., vol. 1, Prol. I. section vi. 18.)

Extraordinary statements these from a writer who is usually so sensible and so accurate. Whether any inspiration other than verbal inspiration is possible, is a problem of metaphysics, and I am not going to discuss it here. Neither shall I defend any "verbal-inspiration theory." What concerns us is the fact of inspiration, so plainly taught by the Lord Himself. And as we have seen in a previous chapter, the fact of inspiration is consistent with sometimes insisting upon the exact words of Scripture with a definiteness so minute that men would call it "hairsplitting," and in other instances quoting Scripture in a way that men would call "loose." Whatever human theories of inspiration may demand, verbal inspiration does not assume that "each Evangelist has recorded the exact words of the inscription," but that the record as given by each was guided and controlled by the Spirit of God. And no one who has studied the human element in other Divine miracles will be surprised at finding a human element in this miracle of inspiration.

But to resume. Each of the four Gospels gives the inscription in a slightly different form. Here is the text of each:—

"This is Jesus, the King of the Jews" (Matt . 27:37).
"The King of the Jews" (Mark 15:26).
"This is the King of the Jews" (Luke 23:38).
"Jesus of Nazareth, the King of the Jews" (John19:19).

Now let us assume, for the sake of argument, that the full inscription was, "This is Jesus of Nazareth, the King of the Jews." Its purpose was clear — not in the least to identify the accused, but solely to give the accusation on which he was condemned. Pilate would not have noticed the charges which so excited the religious leaders of the Jews; but the claim to be a King they represented as a political offence. And though he saw that the prisoner was no rioter, no leader of sedition, and that the accusation was dishonestly preferred, he feared lest the Sanhedrim should make trouble for him with Caesar if he refused to entertain it. [1] Therefore he yielded to their clamor. But he revenged himself upon them by putting up the charge in a form that brought them into contempt, giving prominence to the royal title. Their remonstrance was most noteworthy. "Write not 'The King of the Jews,' but that He said, 'I am King of the Jews.'" [2] And this, which alone was essential, or important, all the Gospels agree in giving.

    1] John 19:12.

    1] John 19:21.

But this is not all. "The title over the cross was written in Greek." If Dean Alford's words are to be judged as the Bible is judged, this statement is a sheer blunder. "The title" was written in Hebrew and Greek and Latin; and this is probably the explanation of the whole matter. "The Hebrew Gospel" might be expected to record the Hebrew inscription. Luke, writing for a Roman officer, would, not unnaturally, reproduce the Latin. [1] The inscription as given by John may well be the Greek. And Mark gives merely, as his words imply, the gist of the charge— "the inscription of the accusation."

> 1] "This is the King of the Jews" has a distinctly Latin ring.

I have dealt thus fully with this matter in spite of the fact that I am personally unable to sympathize with people who find a difficulty in differences of the kind. Such differences only prove that the Gospels are not, as the critics would tell us, copied from one another, or from a common source, but that they are wholly independent narratives. And they weigh nothing with people who have any practical knowledge of men, or who have intelligent views of inspiration. For nothing tends more to discredit witnesses than mechanical uniformity of statement; and in revelation, as in nature, we may expect to find endless variety of detail combined with absolute unity in essentials.

In conclusion, I will deal with a difficulty of a totally different character. But it is important enough to deserve a chapter to itself. The three first Gospels, we are told, are at variance with the fourth, as to the day on which the Lord was crucified.

Chapter 18

The reader will do well to skip this chapter. If it were written to prove Scripture to be wrong, it would be interesting; and, moreover, it would betoken "culture," and might even attract the notice of the newspapers. But as its object is merely to defend Holy Writ on a subject about which enough has been written against it to fill a bookcase, it is really not worth reading.

The first three Gospels agree that the Lord's Supper was instituted at the Jewish Passover on the night before the Crucifixion. [1] Here is Matthew's testimony: —

> 1] Theories of an "anticipatory celebration" by the Lord and His disciples on the 13th Nisan, or a deferred celebration by the leaders of the Jews on the 15th, are preposterous. Here I will but refer my readers to Dr. Edersheim's *Life and Times of the Messiah*, a book which ought to be an "end of controversy" on the subject of the present chapter.

"On the first day of unleavened bread the disciples came to Jesus, saying, Where wilt thou that we make ready for Thee to eat the Passover?" Not "the first day of the Feast" as the A.V. gives it, but the day on which leaven was put away, namely, the 14th Nisan. Mark and Luke state even more explicitly that it was the day when the Passover was killed. (Matt. 26:17; Mark 24:12; Luke 22:7)

But, we are told, "It appears from John 18:28 that on the Friday morning the Jews who conducted our Lord to the pretorium had not yet eaten the Passover." That day, therefore, must have been the 14th Nisan. And this is confirmed by the fact that the Evangelist calls it "the preparation of the Passover" and adds that the following day "was a high day," [1] which proves that it must have been the Feast day, or 15th Nisan. [2]

> 1] John 19:14, 31.
>
> 2] In Hastings's *Bible Dictionary* (vol. 2, p. 634), Prof. Sanday, after noticing that the Synoptists identify the Last Supper with the Passover, goes on to say, "St. John, on the other hand, by a number of clear indications (John 13:1; 18:28; 19:14, 31), implies that the Last Supper was eaten before the time of the regular Passover, and that the Lord suffered on the afternoon of Nisan 14." Prof. Cheyne's *Encyclopedia Biblica* says, "The Synoptists put the Crucifixion on Friday the 15th Nisan, John on Friday the 14th " (article "Chronology," p. 806).

Now at this stage I do not ask that the Evangelists shall be believed as men who were inspired, nor that their writings shall be accepted as Divine oracles, but only that they shall be treated as intelligent and trustworthy witnesses are treated in our courts of justice. Three of them agree in giving a clear and explicit account of certain facts; while the fourth uses language which appears to some to conflict with that of the others. The first question, therefore, would be whether either the competence or the truthfulness of any of them is open to suspicion. And to this the answer is an emphatic negative. The circumstances, moreover, veto the suggestion of a mistake; for the events of those dreadful days must have been burned into the memories of all who took part in them. This being so, the point upon which any tribunal would fix attention would be whether the evidence of the witness that seems to differ from the rest may not have been misconstrued.

I seize upon that point. And my contention is not that, by straining words or having recourse to far-fetched explanations, the last Gospel can be twisted into agreement with the others; but that the exegesis which makes it differ from them is in every part of it a tangle of blunders. For as Lange says, "If the expressions of John be pondered in their full significance, he will be found to have declared more accurately than the rest of the Evangelists that [the Lord] Jesus was crucified on a Friday, and that it was on the first day of the [Feast of the] Passover (viz., on the 15th Nisan)." [1]

> 1] *Life of Christ*, pt. 6, sect. 2.

First and chiefest among the blunders which mark this controversy is that of confounding the Passover with the Feast of Unleavened Bread. Just as the Feast of Weeks came to be known as Pentecost, so the earlier feast was popularly called the Passover. [1] But no intelligent and devout Jew would confound the Supper with the Feast. The language of the Law is clear, "In the fourteenth day of the first month at even is the Lord's passover; and on the fifteenth day of the same month is the feast of unleavened bread." [2]

1] See Luke 22:1, and cf. *Josephus*, Ant. 14:2, 1, and 17:9,3.

2] Lev. 23:5, 6; Numb, 28:16, 17.

Bearing this in mind, we open John 13. The scene is laid at the Paschal Supper, before the Feast of the Passover [1] —that is, on the eve of the festival. And when Judas went out, the disciples supposed he was gone to buy what was needed for the feast (ver. 29). The feast was a Sabbath, when trading was unlawful; but to make provision for all that was needful for the feast was lawful on the preceding night. [2] For yet another blunder is the assumption that always and for all purposes the Jewish day began in the evening. [3] The Passover was eaten during the evening of the 14th Nisan; the feast day began the following morning.

1] We must distinguish this from such passages as Matt. 26:17, where the A.V. wrongly introduces the word "feast."

2] Edersheim's *Life and Times of Messiah*, vol. 2, p. 508.

3] One source of error here is the assumption that either the modern Jewish calendar or practice is the same as in the days of the Ministry.

The weekly Sabbath was reckoned from evening to evening. And every day was so reckoned for purposes of ceremonial cleansing— a fact which enables us to detect another of the blunders of this theory. Ceremonial defilement lapsed at sundown. [1] Therefore, as the Paschal Supper was not eaten until the evening, the Jew would not have been precluded from partaking, by reason of his having entered the Pretorium early in the day. Not so, however, with the holy offerings of the feast day, [2] which were eaten before evening. The only question, therefore, is whether partaking of them could properly be described as "eating the Passover." The law of Moses supplies the answer — "Thou shalt sacrifice the Passover unto the Lord thy God of the flock and the herd . . . seven days shalt thou eat unleavened bread therewith." [3]

>1] Lev. 22:7.
>
>2] The *Chagigah* of the Talmud.
>
>3] Deut. 16:2, 3, cf. 2 Chron. 35:7, 8.

And further still. The Pharisees planned the betrayal on the night of the Supper, because they feared a riot if they seized the Lord upon the day of the Feast. [1] For the suggestion that it was unlawful to be out of doors on that night is due to confounding the law of the Passover in Egypt with the law of the annual celebration.

>1] Matt. 26:5; Mark 14:1, 2.

But the day of the crucifixion was "the preparation of the Passover;" [1] and must not this mean the day before the Passover? My answer is that not a single writer, sacred or profane, can be quoted in support of such a view. "The preparation" was a term in common use among the Jews to describe the day before the weekly Sabbath. It is so used by each of the Evangelists, and by none more definitely than the Fourth, in this very chapter. Every Friday was "the preparation"; this particular Friday was "the Passover preparation." [2]

>1] John 19:14.
>
>2] See Matt, 27:62; Mark 15:42; Luke 23:54; and John 19:31 and 42. Josephus (Ant. 16:6) cites an imperial edict relieving the Jews from appearing before the tribunals either on the Sabbath or after the ninth hour of preparation day. This term was so universally used that it even passed into the Christian Church; and in his note on Mark 15:42, Dean Alford quotes Bishop Wordsworth as saying that it is "the name by which Friday is now generally known in Asia and Greece." See also his note on Matt. 27:62.

One point still remains: "that Sabbath was a high day." [1] True; for not only was it, as being the Sabbath of Passover week, one of the greatest Sabbaths of the year, but further, as being the second day of the Feast, it was kept by the Jews as "the day of the First-fruits" — one of the "red-letter days" in the calendar.

    1] John 19:31.

And now I will turn away to criticisms of another kind, far higher than any of which the Higher Critics take cognizance. Men would be happy in this world if only they could shut out God. And every human religion is designed as a sort of backsheesh to appease or please the Deity. But the Divine religion of Judaism was for a redeemed and happy people; and its special characteristic was a series of festivals—seasons of national rejoicing. The month Nisan began the sacred year; [1] and in that month the first great festival was celebrated—the Feast of Unleavened Bread, or of Passover. One of the rites pertaining to it was the cutting of the first sheaf of the ripened grain, and presenting it in the Temple. During the seven succeeding weeks the entire grain harvest was garnered; and then took place the "Feast of Harvest," or as it was commonly called, of Pentecost. But in Palestine the harvest of the trees was as important as that of the field; and in the autumn, when all had been gathered in, was celebrated the "Feast of In-gathering," or of Tabernacles — the great "harvest-home" of the nation. Feasts they were, and the people were called upon "to rejoice" as they celebrated them. All human religion is marked by sadness: in the harmony of the Divine religion the ruling note was joy. [2]

> 1] Before the Exodus it was the seventh month (Exod. 12:2), a position it still holds in the civil year.
>
> 2] The law of the Feasts will be found in Exod. 23:14-17; Lev. 23; and Deut. 16:1-17.

The first great festival immediately followed the Paschal Supper; the last, the Day of Atonement. For all true worship and all real joy begin with, and are based upon, redemption and forgiveness. The sacred calendar was thus intended as a prophecy; and every part of it has its fulfilment in the great reconciliation. Holy Writ teaches expressly that the Sheaf of the Firstfruits prefigured the resurrection of Christ. Its acceptance was the public proof of the Divine blessing upon the harvest, and the pledge that all would be safely garnered. And so, in the antitype, the resurrection of Christ is the pledge and proof that all His people shall, like Him, be raised — "Christ the first-fruits; afterward they that are Christ's, at His coming." [1]

> 1] 1 Cor. 15:23. The words are ἐγ τῃ παρονίᾳ αὐτοῦ. It is not an isolated event, but the time of His presence as contrasted with this, the time of His absence.

But in the post-captivity revival, the Jews misread the long-neglected law, and in error appointed the day after the feast day, instead of "the morrow after the Sabbath," for the presenting of the first-fruits. And thus it came about that the Lord was lying in the grave upon the very day the rite was celebrated which prefigured His resurrection from the dead. That rite belongs not to the Sabbath, but to "the morrow after the Sabbath" —not to the seventh day, which was the "rest" of the old creation, but to "the first day of the week," the rest-day of that new creation of which He is the Firstborn and the Head. [1]

> 1] Deut. 16:9 makes it clear that the day of the first-fruits was not to be a Sabbath, and that the Divine intention was that a sheaf of corn, cut that very day, should be carried to the Temple and waved before the Lord. And it follows, of course, that the true day of Pentecost (which in that year was observed upon a Sabbath) must always be the first day of the week—a fact which confirms the presumption that it was when assembled on the Lord's Day that the Church received the gift of the Holy Ghost. It is held by some that the ambiguous word employed in Acts 2:1 means "fulfilled" in the sense of passed (*Smith's Bible Dic.*, "Pentecost," vol. 2, p. 786).

The seeming fitness of assigning the death of Christ to the very day the Paschal lamb was killed has weight with many. [1] But this is owing to the almost exclusive prominence which popular theology accords to that most popular of types. The offerings of the opening chapters of Leviticus [2] have a still larger place in the doctrinal teaching of the New Testament [3]; and these great sacrifices of the law marked the feast day on which the Lord was crucified. [4]

> 1] To suppose it occurred at the same hour is a blunder. The lamb was killed "between the evenings," i.e., between the sun's decline and its final disappearance—about 6 p.m. (Edersheim, 2:490).

2] The burnt-offering with its meat-offering, the peace-offering (the *Chagigah* of the Talmud) and the sin-offering (Lev. 1-4.).

3] In Hebrews, e.g., the offerings of the law are prominently mentioned, while the Passover has no place in the doctrine of the Epistle.

4] Numb. 28:17-23. (Comp. Josephus, Ant. 3:10, 5.)

Other synchronisms, too, there were. The greatest mystery of the Passion was not His suffering from men, but His being forsaken of God. In a real sense, indeed, the sufferings inflicted upon Him by men were but a consequence of this. Hence His reply to Pilate, "Thou couldest have no power at all against Me, except it were given thee from above." If men seized and slew Him, it was because God had delivered Him up. "This is your hour and the power of darkness," He exclaimed in Gethsemane. And not till that destined hour had struck was the Almighty Hand withdrawn which till then had shielded Him from outrage. His death was the close, and not the beginning, of His sufferings: in truth it was the hour of His triumph.

The yearly Passover was merely a memorial of the Passover in Egypt; and the midnight agony in Gethsemane was the great antitype of that midnight scene when the destroying angel flashed through the land of the Pharaohs. And as His death was the accomplishment of His people's deliverance, it took place upon the anniversary of "that selfsame day that the Lord did bring the children of Israel out of the land of Egypt." [1] And that day again was a great anniversary: it was "the selfsame day" of the covenant with Abraham. [2]

1] Exod. 12:51.

2] Ibid., verse 41. The day of the resurrection was also an anniversary. On the 17th day of the month Nisan (or Abib) the renewed earth emerged from the waters of the Flood (Gen. 8:4); the redeemed people emerged from the waters of the sea, and the Lord Jesus Christ rose from the dead.

As we have seen, then, the Sacred Calendar of Israel is a prophecy of redemption. In the Temple there was the inner shrine within the second veil, where none but the High Priest might ever enter; the holy place, into which the priests might come; and the court without, where all the people could approach. And in redemption we have the same threefold division: first the Christ, and those who, as "partakers of the heavenly calling," have, in Him, the right of nearest access; secondly, the earthly people, yet to become a kingdom of priests; and, thirdly, the great multitude of the redeemed of earth. And so here. The sheaf of the first fruits in its primary interpretation stands for Christ alone. But the prophecy of the Calendar, like many another prophecy, has a double fulfilment; and, in its secondary application, that sheaf represents not merely the personal Christ, but the official Christ, including all who share "the heavenly calling." [1] And the wave loaves of Pentecost represent the earthly people, as such, in their special place of privilege and blessing.

> 1] "The heavenly calling" is not limited to "the Church which is His body"—the special election of the present dispensation; it includes also the Bride—a special election out of Israel in the dispensation to follow. John the Baptist—the last great prophet of the earthly people—speaks of the Bride (John 3:29); and then the Bride disappears from Scripture, to reappear in Rev. 19:7, 21:9 ff., which relate to the restoration of the earthly people. But Christian theology *more suo* appropriates all Israel's blessings, the bridal glory not excepted, and with exemplary discrimination apportions the curses to the Jews! Holy Scripture nowhere speaks of the Church of this dispensation as the bride; and Eph. 5:25-33 asserts by implication that it is not. To appeal to 2 Cor. 11:2 is mere trifling.

But the covenant promise to Abraham included blessing for all the nations of the earth. This is in the book of the beginnings — the book of Genesis; and in the visions of the Revelation, the book of the endings, we read of the elect Pentecostal company of the redeemed of Israel on earth, and then of the palm-bearing multitude of the Feast of Tabernacles — "a great multitude which no man could number, of all nations and kindreds, and people and tongues." [1]

> 1] Gen. 22:18, Rev. 7:3-9. (The carrying of branches of palm trees marked the Feast of Tabernacles, Lev. 23:40.) And compare Rev. 14:1-6. The scene here again is laid on earth. First we have the 144,000 of the redeemed of Israel; and their promised blessing is followed by the proclamation of "the everlasting gospel" to "every nation, and kin-

dred, and tongue, and people." Zech. 14 gives the result in plain, prosaic words.

This is not a wild inference from isolated texts It is the burden of prophecy as a whole. The present dispensation, we are expressly told, is typified by the first of the sacred festivals. "Our passover has been sacrificed, even Christ," says the Apostle in enjoining holiness of life, "wherefore let us keep the feast." [1] And the true Pentecost is yet to come. The great event of the Church's baptism, as recorded in the Acts, was within the scope of Joel's prophecy, [2] but it was not the fulfilment of it. That belongs to those wonderful and awful days of mingled blessing and judgment, which are to herald "the times of the restitution of all things"—the period of the last great festival, the Feast of Tabernacles.

> 1] 1 Cor. 5:7, 8 (R.V.) The subject here is, not the Eucharist, but the Christian life on earth.
>
> 2] Joel 2:28-3:2. Mark the language of the inspired Apostle in Acts ii. 16. In the accuracy of Scripture a distinction is often made between events which are within the scope of a prophecy and events which fulfil it.

For the "restoration of all things" is not, as some would tell us, the accomplishment in eternity of a scheme, now secret, to bring all the lost to heaven. It is the realization upon earth, and in days which shall yet be marked and measured in human calendars, of a Divine purpose plainly declared upon the open page of Scripture. Of these "times of restoration " the inspired Apostle tells us, "God hath spoken by the mouth of all His holy prophets since the world began." And to make it more emphatic still, he adds, "Yea, all the prophets, from Samuel and those that follow after, as many as have spoken, have likewise foretold of these days." In a word, they are the burden of all prophetic testimony, from first to last, in relation to what theologians call "the Second Advent."

In the simple prose of the Epistle to the Romans this same truth is plainly taught. The "fall" of Israel has proved "the riches of the world"; the setting aside of Israel, "the reconciling of the world." What then, the Apostle asks, shall be their restoration to favor but "life from the dead"? Mark the force and meaning of these words. When the coming Pentecost — the presentation to God of the "two wave loaves" of Israel and Judah restored to Divine favor and blessing—leads on to the last great Feast of Ingathering, results will be achieved on a scale so vast and wonderful that, in contrast with them, the greatest present-day successes in evangelizing the world will seem like death. In comparison with the Feast of Passover the Feast of Tabernacles — that coming triumph of redemption — will be "as life from the dead."

But in the great mass of critical literature all this is absolutely ignored. And yet it is but the realization of the prayer, "Thy will be done on earth as it is done in heaven" —words which are daily uttered as an incantation by multitudes of people who regard the hope of their fulfilment as a dream of fanatics.

Even that poor type of Evangelicalism whose horizon of truth is narrowed to what might be described as the Police Court Gospel which tells how Christ has paid the sinner's penalty, stands on a vastly higher level than the mere religionist, with his "carnal ordinances," not omitting ritual and millinery. But such teachers, one and all, leave us an easy prey to rationalistic critics. For while they vehemently assert that the Bible is the Word of God, they use it merely as a book of piety or of religion.

The story is told of one who hid himself in the library of a famous German theologian of the eighteenth century, that he might learn the secret of his fellowship with God. Let us thus take the place of eavesdroppers upon the Apostle of the Gentiles as he writes his great Redemption treatise. He first unfolds the wonders of grace in the gospel. Then he turns aside to mark how every Divine scheme of blessing for man on earth has been baffled by human sin. And lastly he goes on to show how this tale of apostasy and ruin is but a dark background for the display of a supreme purpose which is to include the fulfilment of all that has thus seemingly been thwarted and lost. And having thus reached the climax of the revelation entrusted to him for the Church, nothing remains but to enforce by exhortation and appeal a life of holiness and righteousness befitting those who are recipients of such "mercies." But ere he turns the page he exclaims in adoration, "O the depth of the riches both of the wisdom and knowledge of God! how unsearchable are His judgments and His ways past finding out. For of Him, and through Him, and to Him are all things: to Him be the glory forever. Amen."

Chapter 19

This book has already passed the limits I had fixed for it; and though I seem to have but touched the fringe of a subject which is inexhaustible, the present chapter must be the last.

Here, then, is my answer to the question of the opening page, Whether, in view of modern criticism, the Bible may still be received with the settled and simple faith accorded to it in the past? "I hold no man's proxy," and yet in a sense I represent a class that may surely claim a right to be heard in this controversy. Taught in early life to regard the Bible as the inspired Word of God, we came in time to feel the power of destructive criticism. And our faith was severely tested by the strain. For the man who believes on mere human testimony that a virgin bore a child, and that a dead man came back to life, is a superstitious creature who would believe anything.

The question at issue, therefore, is between agnosticism and Christianity. And we have faced that question in the light of all that the critics have to urge. Some of us have studied the Bible quite as diligently as they have; and as the result, while wholly free from the trammels of "articles" and "creeds," we have come back to the faith of those who framed those formularies. We do not look upon the martyrs with patronizing pity as fanatics or fools. The faith they died for we deem worth living for. And if belief in Holy Scripture in the sense in which they believed in it led to the same consequences now as in dark days gone by, we trust we should not shrink from them.

My answer, then, is clear and unequivocal. As for the manner of it I am well aware of its faults and imperfections. But one characteristic of it, for which I expect to be taken severely to task, I refuse to regard as a fault at all. At the outset I waived appeals to authority, and therefore I have deliberately abstained from paying the critical scholars the homage to which they are accustomed. To adopt the words of Dr. Pusey, "I have turned against skeptic s their own weapons, and used ridicule against the would be arguments of a false criticism which thought itself 'free' because it made free with God's Word." [1]

1] Dr. Pusey's Daniel (Preface).

My treatment of the critics is due to no want of deference for scholarship. But that which gives them such a commanding influence upon the public mind is not their scholarship, but the vantage-ground they occupy as professors of Christian universities or colleges, or ministers of Christian Churches. Their power to attack the Bible is mainly due to positions they have gained by giving solemn pledges to defend it. Not that I accuse them of conscious dishonesty in this. They are above the suspicion of such a charge. But they do not view things as others view them. The morality of religious men seems to differ from that of ordinary men. The critics see no inconsistency between their position and their teaching; just as they cannot see the obvious consequences of that teaching. Moreover, with some notable exceptions, they are mere experts, and experts are proverbially lacking in judgment.

To speak in this way of such eminent personages will seem to some people almost to savor of profanity. Many of us have laughed over David Ross's warning to his wife in *The Days of Auld Lang Syne*, [Gaelic] "We maun be cannie wi' John's title, wumman, for ye ken professor is a by-ordinar' word: a' count it equal tae earl at the verra least, an' it wudna dae tae be aye usin't." But in this controversy we cannot afford to be "cannie." The issues at stake are too tremendous. And moreover, nothing sublunary is sacred to a lawyer.

I may plead, too, that I have merely brought the critics within the meshes of their own net. I have treated them as they themselves treat the "Biblical writers." Appeals to the New Testament they refuse on the ground that the inspired Apostles of the Lord, and even the Lord Himself, were prejudiced and ignorant: is it very shocking, then, to question their own competency? As for me, I would say, in borrowed language, how deeply I feel my "utter weakness before the power of His Word and my inability to sound the depths even of its simplest sentence." But yet it would be the merest affectation in one who knows even a little of the spiritual meaning and "hidden harmony" of Scripture, to pretend that he can study such works as Hastings's *Bible Dictionary* and The *Encyclopedia Biblica* without being conscious of living in a sphere which most of the writers seem to have never entered, and of the very existence of which they display no knowledge.

It will be said perhaps that in these books the editors and contributors write avowedly as critics, and it is not fair to assume that they are only critics. But can any one point to anything that has come from their facile pens which gives proof of acquaintance with the spiritual power of Holy Scripture as "the living and eternally abiding Word of God"? (1 Pet. 1:23.) [1]

> 1] "Robertson Smith," exclaims a friend at my elbow. "Oh the pity of it!" is my rejoinder; for I recall such words as these: "Only of this I am sure at the outset, that the Bible does speak to the heart of man in words that can only come from God" (Old Testament in the Jewish Church). But see p. 39, ante. And one of the most notable of his successors in Scotland is now running the same course; so that Professor Cheyne need no longer pity his weakness (*Old Testament Criticism*, p. 245).

"It is the first rule of criticism," one of the most eminent and trusted of the critics tells us, "that a good critic must be a good interpreter of the thoughts of his author"; [1] and it would be difficult to frame a sentence which more definitely discredits the whole fraternity. "These are they which bear witness of Me" [2] is the Divine inscription upon the Hebrew Scriptures; and in ignoring this the critics are entirely out of touch with the thoughts both of the God who inspired the Bible and of its human authors.

> 1] Robertson Smith, *Old Testament in the Jewish Church*, Lecture III.
>
> 2] John 5:39 (R.V.)

Our quarrel with the Higher Criticism, I repeat with emphasis, is not because it is criticism, but because it is purely destructive, and therefore the lowest kind of criticism. And, moreover, it systematically ignores the science of evidence, on which all true criticism rests. In fact, when judged by every test that can be applied to it, it is found wanting.

In the higher sense of the word a "critic" is a skilled and impartial judge — all that here in England we expect a judge to be. Its secondary meaning is that of "a harsh examiner," a hostile faultfinder. These skeptical writers belong to the second category. And let this be kept in view. We do not reject the ascertained results of true criticism. Our protest is against the assumptions of a criticism which is unsound in principle, and which is carried on by unsound methods. "We are prepared as Christian men to receive and welcome the fullest light of the new learning. We are not prepared to be dragged at the wheels of those who would give us a discredited Old Testament, an emasculated New Testament, a fallible Christ." [1]

> 1] These words are quoted from Dr. Sinker's valuable treatise on *The Higher Criticism* (p. 184).

If therefore I may venture to combine practical counsel with this summary and retrospect, I would say, first, let no one be "browbeaten out of belief" by these attacks upon Holy Scripture. The Bible is not discredited because eminent scholars have turned against it in the camp of faith. The critics represent indeed that the scholarship of Christendom is with them. But the claim is absolutely unfounded. [1] Their apparent preeminence is due largely to their being adepts in the art of what the Americans call "literary logrolling." They are "a mutual admiration society." No one of them can raise a cry but that the whole party responds. And then the secular Press joins in. For the Press is with them. Naturally. For the newspapers represent "the world," and "the world" is never on the side of Divine truth.

> 1] Such a book as *Lex Mosaica* is in itself an answer to it that notable work is a complete refutation of the critical attack upon the Pentateuch.

The alarming spread of skepticism among the Nonconformists during the last quarter of a century has been largely due to their wincing under this charge of want of scholarship. They long refused to barter the faith of Christ for German rationalism. But Matthew Arnold's appeal for "culture" was a veiled taunt which they keenly felt; and like the schoolboy who is shamed into evil ways by the fear of being deemed unmanly, they betook themselves to the new cult. Under this influence many of the younger men are now ministers of "culture," instead of being ministers of the gospel. The result is that while, politically and socially, Nonconformity never stood higher, as a spiritual power it has sensibly declined. It is bartering its birthright for a mess of pottage.

It is noteworthy that this boast of a monopoly of scholarship, and this taunt of want of culture, were among the weapons used by the Arians in the supreme controversy of early days. Those who stood with Athanasius in the great struggle for the faith of Christ appeared for a time to be a weak minority. But the undeclared suffrages of "the whole congregation of Christian people" were behind them; and in the end the truth triumphed.

If I may go on to offer advice of a still more practical kind, I would say in the words of that most sensible of men, the town clerk of Ephesus, "Seeing that these things cannot be gainsaid, ye ought to be quiet." It is idle to hold exciting meetings, and to shout for "about the space of two hours" that the Bible is the Word of God. A reaction is sure to follow; and when the shouting is over thoughtful people will turn away to listen to the critics.

The success of the skeptical movement is not due to the strength of the attack, but to the weakness of the defense. With the vast majority of Christians the Bible is nothing more than "a plan of salvation" and "a book of piety." Of "the riches both of the wisdom and knowledge of God" which it unfolds they are content to know nothing. The golden threads of type and prophecy which are in the warp and woof of it from Genesis to Revelation, they ignore. And some who pose as champions of the Bible share the ignorance of those whom they seek to lead. No wonder, therefore, if skepticism prevails.

I once asked the late Bishop of Limerick, when visiting him in his charming summer home upon the Kenmare river, whether, when separated from his library and his work, the time did not sometimes hang heavily. I well remember Dr. Graves's answer. "Give me," said he, "a single square yard on the side of a dry ditch, and I can find enough to interest me for a day." To me, I confess, a Kerry ditch, wet or dry, would be nothing but a ditch. And there are multitudes "who profess and call themselves Christians" to whom the Bible is nothing but a book. And yet with the spiritually intelligent every page of it will bear the microscope. Not a single student of prophecy can be found in the ranks of the critics; not a single individual who understands the Pentateuch as "the word of the beginning of Christ." [1]

> 1] In other words, the critics know nothing of the typology of Scripture. And therefore they are ignorant of the language in which Christian doctrine is taught in the New Testament.

Let us never forget that the Higher Criticism is what has been called "post-mortem talk." No one could make a constant study of a post-mortem report upon some lost relative or friend without becoming morbid or degraded. And a like deterioration seems to result from the habitual study of the critics. Let us then keep their books on the upper shelf, and use them only for reference. These writers seem to miss even the open and obvious scope of the Old Testament as the Divine history of the Abrahamic race. And its esoteric teaching about Christ, which pervades not merely the writings of the Prophets, but the Law and the "Former Prophets" (as the historical books were called), they entirely ignore. And it is neither wholesome nor even safe for the Christian to accustom himself to a system of Bible study in which Christ has no place. [1]

> 1] "It is ignorance of Christ which turns the Scriptures into a dark, inexplicable riddle." — Birks's *Modern Rationalism*.

Here I would add a warning against being frightened by a parade of seeming errors in the Scriptures. In the preceding chapters I have selected examples of various classes of difficulties, and have shown how some that may seem to be insoluble can not only be explained, but so explained as to become helps to faith. Others there are, no doubt, to the solution of which we cannot find a clue, though perhaps, if we had all the facts and circumstances in view, the solution might be simple and obvious. But surely it is a poor sort of faith that depends on the absence of difficulties.

Treat your Bible as you would treat your friend. A friendship that cannot bear the strain of a misunderstanding does not deserve the name; nor a faith that gives way in presence of a difficulty. But with many the place the Bible holds resembles that not of a friend at all, but rather that of a mere acquaintance. For proofs that it is the Word of God are clear and abundant. But they do not lie open on the surface. Gold and diamonds are not picked up upon the highway; men need to dig for them. Even Nature hides her treasures from the trifler.

God is "a rewarder of them that seek Him diligently."

But nothing is gained by exaggeration or overstatement. When, adopting the language of Scripture itself, we call it the Word of God, the oracles of God, we make full allowance for possible errors in transcription, and imperfection in translation. But as we have seen, to press these considerations to a point that would impair its Divine authority betokens perverseness and pedantry.

And this leads me to repeat a warning against identifying the fact of inspiration with any definition of it, or with popular theories respecting it. Many people, for instance, seem to assume that we cannot regard Genesis as inspired unless it be maintained that every portion of it was imparted to Moses in the same way that the 53rd chapter of Isaiah was imparted to the prophet. But what warrant is there for this? If the Higher Criticism view of Exodus, for example, be sustained, that book is a profane fraud, and our Divine Lord is an unreliable teacher. But if the *a priori* argument in favor of a written revelation be valid, it vetoes the assumption that there was no such revelation during the thousands of years which preceded the Mosaic age. That Genesis was based on existing "documents" is a reasonable suggestion; but the inference that this disproves its claim to inspiration is false. Our Lord set His seal upon the book as a whole, but He said no word either to guide or to restrain the efforts of reverent and competent criticism to analyze it.

While therefore the absence of definitions and theories will seem to some a serious defect in this book, it is a defect which I refuse to remedy. If any one doubts whether God could make His will known to men, unmistakably, and in language they can understand, the question at issue is not inspiration at all, but the power and character of God. And while an intelligent skepticism will apply the severest tests to anything claiming to be a Divine revelation, the rejection of it on *a priori* grounds is nothing but the dull stupidity of an ignorant unbelief.

The Higher Criticism is, as we have seen, the product, not of nineteenth century enlightenment, but of eighteenth century rationalism. And yet it can boast of a far more venerable origin. For while there is plenty that is novel in its elaborate details, in its main outlines there is nothing new. People talk as though the faith of the Church as to Holy Scripture was settled in an uncritical and ignorant age when the objections and difficulties which now influence the minds of men were unknown. The thought is worthy of this conceited age of ours. The faith of the Church was settled under a fire of keen and intelligent criticism. Names such as Celsus and Porphyry, and the rest, not to speak of the Gnostics and other sects, will occur to every student. The "Mosaic narrative" was, then as now, explained as allegory, or dismissed as fable. The Mosaic books were declared not to be Mosaic at all, but the product of a later time. The historical books were discredited as being unauthentic, and the miracles were ridiculed. And in the case of such books as Jonah and Daniel it may be averred that the modern attack adds nothing that will stand the test of still more modern discoveries. The distinctive element in the Higher Criticism is merely that the attack is now delivered from the Christian camp.

And in conclusion I would repeat with emphasis a warning against being deceived as to the significance of the present movement. There is nothing which proves more plainly a critic's want of judgment, and of clearness of vision, than the incapacity to see that the Christ controversy of the Early Church is reopened by the Bible controversy of today. A supernatural creed which does not rest on a supernatural foundation is not faith, but superstition. Puzzle - headed people may taunt us with putting the Bible in the place of Christ, but every clear thinker recognizes that once we pass out of the sphere where reason and the senses can teach us, we are dependent absolutely on a Divine revelation.

Not that "the historic Jesus" is a myth. The rejection of the Evangelists' testimony betokens not a reasonable skepticism, but the stupidity of the "boot-eating" juror, who doggedly refuses to believe the evidence. But an intelligent appreciation of the evidence for the public facts of His life and ministry stands quite apart from belief in the Divinity of Christ. The foundation truth of Christianity is that the Man of Calvary is now sitting upon the throne of God. And I appeal to all fair minds whether I am not justified in saying that those who believe this upon no better authority than the Higher Critics' Bible are credulous and superstitious. We can reach the Living Word only through the written Word. Therefore in contending for a really inspired — an absolutely authoritative — Bible, we can say with Athanasius, "We are fighting for our all." [1]

> 1] It is a well-known fact that the present dearth of candidates for Holy Orders is due, not to the causes publicly put

> forward, but to the effects of the Higher Criticism in undermining faith in the Incarnation among those who might be expected to offer themselves for ordination. And it would be a rash statement at this moment to assert that the majority of the clergy believe the Apostles' Creed. The book *Contenlio Veritatis*, by "Six Oxford Tutors," bears startling testimony to the extent of the present apostasy. Those of the writers who clearly believe in the supernatural appear to do so as Churchmen and not as Christians.

But it is not merely in this incidental way that the Higher Criticism undermines the foundations of Christianity. It attacks them directly. The critics freely acknowledge that the Lord Jesus Christ accredited the Old Testament as being the Word of God. Unless, therefore, they can discredit His testimony their whole position must be condemned as not only false, but profane. And from this, as we have seen, they do not shrink.

The Christian truth of the Humiliation is that, with the full realization of all that He was, and the clear apprehension of all that God had revealed in the Scriptures which testified of Him, the Lord in infinite grace stooped to the lowest depths of self-emptying and self-effacement. But the Kenosis of this new theology betokens not Divine grace but human misfortune. It is not the humiliation of Christ, but His degradation. It is not that He became man, but that He sank to the level of a Jew of that age. Not that while "knowing that the Father had given all things into His hands and that He was come from God and was going to God," [1] He humbled Himself; but that knowing nothing more than His contemporaries, His mind was warped by prejudice and ignorance. [2]

> 1] John 13:3.
>
> 2] This is merely a summary of the argument of chap. 6.

Such is the doctrine of the critics on this question of transcendent importance. Nor is it an excrescence upon their theology that might be got rid of: it is vital to their system. They admit that they are challenging what has been the belief of the Church in all ages. They admit that that false belief—as they deem it—is based upon the teaching of the Lord Jesus Christ. Their whole position, therefore, is untenable unless they can disparage His authority or His competence.

It is clear, therefore, that the Higher Criticism raises again in a new and more subtle phase the same issue as the old Arian heresy. It is not the Bible that is at stake, but the Christ of the Bible. Is it, then, the language of exaggeration to declare that in resisting it "we are fighting for our all"?

Appendix

Note I
(Chap.6.)
Isolated Texts Relied On By The Higher Critics.

It is notorious that great heresies are generally based on isolated texts, and the rationalistic attack on the Pentateuch relies on a perversion of Exodus 6:3 and Jeremiah 7:22.

The former passage is used by the critics to prove that the name "Jehovah" was unknown to the Patriarchs. It is droll how these men employ arguments which refute themselves; for if the book be a literary forgery it is certain that the brilliant author of it would not have given himself away like this.

Most of the Tubingen heresies have an element of truth in them, and the figment that Jehovah was the tribal deity of Israel is a travesty of the truth that this was God's covenant name — His name in relation to His people as brought into covenant relationship with Himself. To Abraham the covenant was a promise; it was not till four centuries afterwards that it was established as a public fact. The Patriarchs received private revelations, but now He was about to declare Himself openly. Hence His words in Exodus 6 — "Thou shalt see what I will do to Pharaoh." And He adds, "I am Jehovah; and I appeared unto Abraham, unto Isaac, and unto Jacob, as God Almighty, but as to My name Jehovah I was not known to them" (R.V., margin). The significance of that name was never known until (as He goes on to say) He "remembered" His covenant; that is, until the time had come for Him in fulfilment of it to deliver His people from their sojournings and their bondage. "Wherefore, say unto the children of Israel, I am Jehovah" (ver. 6).

Jeremiah 7:22 reads: "I spake not unto your fathers, nor commanded them in the day that I brought them out of the land of

Egypt, concerning burnt-offerings or sacrifices." And this is taken as proof that "the Levitical Code" was not in existence in Jeremiah's day.

Such a perversion of the prophet's words would be impossible but for the prevailing ignorance of the teaching of the Pentateuch. To the intelligent Christian they appear to be merely a bare statement of a fact which is plain upon the open page of the Book of Exodus. The prophet adds, "But this thing commanded I them, saying, Obey My voice, and I will be your God, and ye shall be My people." This was the burden of all the Divine teaching at the Exodus. When God brought Israel out of Egypt there was not even a suggestion of the Levitical code of sacrifices. That was promulgated after the formal dedication of the covenant, as a Divine provision to maintain Israel in the position already assured to them as a redeemed and holy people. And its significance was twofold. Its esoteric teaching was of Christ. Its outward value was solely as a test of obedience. But when, in the pre-exilic apostasy, the Jews made it a mere religion, and put it in the place of heart-obedience to God, it became only a curse to them.

I will risk a charge of egotism by referring here to Chapter 12 of my *Buddha of Christendom*. I do so, however, because, though it affords a refutation of this error of the critics, it was written without any reference to the Pentateuch controversy.

Note II
(Chap. 8.)
The Revised Version Of The New Testament

I wish to bring in the R.V. controversy only in so far as my argument demands it. The method on which the revisers dealt with the text has been thus described by one of the company (Dr. Newth), whose account is confirmed by Bishop Ellicott himself. The Bishop, as chairman, asked whether any textual changes were proposed. "By tacit consent" Drs. Scrivener and Hort were left to reply by stating their respective views. "Dr. Scrivener opens up the matter by stating the facts of the case and giving his judgment on the bearings of the evidence. Dr. Hort follows, . . . and, if differing from Dr. S.'s estimate of the weight of the evidence, gives his reasons and states his own view. After discussion the vote of the company is taken, and the proposed reading accepted or rejected. The text being thus settled, the chairman asks for proposals on the rendering."

Is it any wonder that a learned writer declared that if this description of their action "is not a kind of joke, it is quite enough to 'settle' this Revised Greek Testament in a very different sense"? Fancy a question of prescriptive rights being "settled" in such a manner as this in a court of justice! And remember that, while "textual criticism" sounds very recondite, the question at issue in every instance was as definitely a matter of evidence as is the case in a suit about a water-course or a right of way. And it ought to have been dealt with according to the established principles and rules of evidence.

If the four or five most ancient MSS. were always in accord a plausible case might be made out for following them to the exclusion of the other authorities. But as a matter of fact they are scarcely ever in accord in any instance where they differ from the Received Text. Suppose that in a prescriptive rights action the "ancient witnesses" called for the plaintiff differed in their evidence, and the jury by a majority vote decided to follow some of them in opposition to the others and also to the united voice of the rest of the community ; and you have in a parable the action of the Revisers in "settling" the Greek text.

And in numberless cases where the Revisers happily refused to mutilate the text, they compromised matters by allowing the insertion in the margin of an alternative reading, which, though possibly quite devoid of authority, suggests a doubt as to the right reading of the passage.

The question of the translation is quite outside the purpose of this reference to the R.V., which is merely to emphasize the fact that skeptical objections based on textual criticism are worthless. I will therefore dismiss the matter with a word of comment and a word of advice.

An old MS. may have survived its fellows for the same reason that an old pair of boots sometimes survives, namely, through having been put aside on account of some fault or blemish. Of the five most ancient MSS. which the Revisers chiefly followed, three are declared by critics of eminence to be corrupt and untrustworthy.

And the advice I venture to offer to readers who cannot revise the R.V. for themselves is this: Read the Gospels always in the Authorized Version, using the R.V. only as a book of reference; and when the text differs, assume that the A.V. is right, for in the great majority of cases it is so.

Note III
(Chap. 11.)
"Three Days And Three Nights"

Some people cannot understand how the Lord's words that He would be "three days and three nights" in the grave could be true if He died on Friday and rose on Sunday morning. This is a notable instance of the common blunder of interpreting words and phrases otherwise than by their use. Words are but counters; they have no intrinsic value. The only practical question, therefore, is What do they stand for? And what alone concerns us here is, What meaning did the Lord's words convey to those to whom they were addressed? To this question the Gospels afford the answer. Four-and twenty hours after His burial the Jews came to Pilate and said, "We remember that that deceiver said, while he was yet alive, *After three days* I will rise again; command therefore that the sepulcher be made sure until the third day" (Matt, 27:63, 64). Compare with this 2 Chron. 10:5-12, relative to the new king and his Israelite subjects. "He said unto them, Come again unto me after three days. . . . So Jeroboam and all the people came to Rehoboam on the third day." Or see Esther 4:16; 5:1. The Queen's order to her people was, "Fast ye for me, and neither eat nor drink, three days, night or day." And yet "On the third day" Esther held the banquet.

In either case the words conveyed to those who used and heard them a meaning different from that which we attach to them. Had Jeroboam not come on the third day it would have meant rebellion. Had that Easter Sunday passed leaving the seal upon the tomb unbroken, the guard would have been withdrawn, and the Pharisees would have proclaimed their triumph.

A prison chaplain would find no difficulty in explaining this to his congregation. Our civil day begins at midnight, and the law reckons any part of a day as a day. Therefore while a sentence of three days means three days of twenty-four hours, equal to seventy-two hours, a prisoner under such a committal is seldom more than forty hours in jail; and I have known cases where the period was in fact only thirty-three hours. And this mode of reckoning and of speaking was as familiar to the Jew as it is to the *habitués* of our criminal courts. "A day and a night make an Onah, and a part of an Onah is as the whole." Dr. Lightfoot quotes this Jewish saying in his *Hora Hebraica* (Matt. 12:40); and he adds: "Therefore Christ may truly be said to have been in his grave three Onoth .... the consent of the schools and the dialect of the nation agreeing thereunto."

I have seen it stated that as Jonah's imprisonment in the whale lasted three days and three nights the Lord must have laid for as long a period in the grave. But this is only another phase of the same blunder. There is no reason to suppose that Jonah's "three days and nights" was a longer period than our Lord's.

Note IV
(Chap. 15)
The Genealogies Of Our Lord

Some people seem to assume that the gospel "Genealogies" were dictated to Matthew and Luke by the Spirit of God: others, that they were based on the gossip of Joseph's family. It is not easy to decide which view is the more extraordinary. These genealogies were of course transcripts of Jewish records; for such pedigrees were a specialty with the Jews, especially in the case of families belonging to the Royal or Priestly houses. And if they had not been authentic they would have been promptly exposed, and the Gospels discredited, by the Jewish opponents of Christianity. As Dr. Bloomfield writes (*Greek Test. Com.*): "If these genealogies of Christ (which must be understood to have been derived from the public records in the temple) had not been agreeable thereto, the deception would have been instantly detected."

This is so obvious that I should not notice it were it not for the use made of these genealogies by certain of the critics. For example, one of the lesser lights, quoted more than once in these pages, referring to the very probable hypothesis that Matthew gives the pedigree of Joseph, and Luke that of Mary, predicts that "a coming generation of Bible students will find it almost incredible that such an explanation should have been seriously urged." He goes on to notice superciliously that "Joseph's family occupied twenty-eight generations, while in the same time Mary's family got through thirty-eight generations ;" and ends, "Luke inadvertently states that Joseph was the son of Heli, when he meant that Mary was the daughter of Heli." This is meant to be very smart. The reader must decide whether such writing does not justify my treatment of the critics. The real question thus raised is not at all the inspiration of the Gospels, but whether the Evangelists are deserving of any attention or respect.

An alternative explanation, that Matthew gives Joseph's genealogy as legal successor to the throne of David, and Luke his private genealogy, is maintained with much erudition and force in Lord Arthur Hervey's *Genealogies of our Lord Jesus Christ*. An epitome of his argument will be found in his article, "Genealogy of Christ," in Smith's Bible Dictionary. A brief notice of the other view will be found in Dean Plumptre's note to Luke 3:23 in Bishop Ellicott's *New Testament Commentary for English Readers*.

Dr. Bullinger states the matter thus:— "Matthew gives the royal and legal line through Solomon; Luke gives the natural and lineal line through Nathan. The former is the line according to legal succession; the latter is the line according to natural descent. . . . Both lines meet in Joseph, the son of Jacob by birth, and the son of Heli by marriage with Mary, Heli's only daughter." [1]

> 1] *Number in Scripture*, p. 159. In a footnote he notices that the verb used in Luke 3:23 means "to own as a custom or usage" (Liddell & Scott). It is not " as was supposed," but " as was reckoned by Jewish customs." (Bloomfield's *Gr. Test.*)

Note V
(Chap. 15)
The Distinction Between The Kingdom Of Heaven, The Kingdom Of God, And The Church.

The term "Kingdom of Heaven," or, to be strictly accurate, "the Kingdom of the Heavens," occurs thirty-three times in the First Gospel, and nowhere else in the New Testament. [1]

> 1] The expression was used by Jewish writers in a vague sense = the inward love and fear of God (Horn Hebraica, Matt. iii. 2).

The Greek work basileia has the same range of meaning as our English word "Kingdom." It means (1) royal authority; sovereign power; rule; or (2) the territory or country over which a king rules. Therefore the Kingdom of the Heavens must mean either (1) the rule of the heavens over the earth, or else (2) the heavens as the scene or sphere of Divine rule. We cannot hesitate in deciding that (1) is the meaning here, "the heavens" standing for "God" by a well-known figure of speech. And our best commentators, recognizing this, refer to the Book of Daniel to explain it; but, having thus found the key, they generally throw it away unused.

"That the heavens do rule" was announced to Nebuchadnezzar as a present fact and truth (Dan. 4:26). But yet the visions of Daniel ii. and vii. foretold a future kingdom —a kingdom in the same sense in which Babylon, Persia, Greece, and Rome were kingdoms — foretold a time when God would take back the scepter of earthly sovereignty which He had entrusted to Nebuchadnezzar. Now this Messianic kingdom is connected in prophecy with the race of Abraham and the throne of David. And the New Testament opens with a revelation of the Lord Jesus Christ as the heir of David and of Abraham — the Messiah of the Promises, the king of Messianic prophecy. And His ministry began by an announcement that the promised rule was about to come. Matt. 3:2 was not the statement of a present truth or fact, but a prophetic declaration. This was the purpose of the First Gospel; and the Holy Spirit so guided and restrained the writer of it that it contains not one single sentence that is inconsistent with that purpose. It is the Gospel of the Kingdom of Heaven; for the expression is peculiar to Matthew, who uses it some thirty-three times, meaning always and only the promised Messianic earthly kingdom.

The expression "the Kingdom of God" occurs five times in Matthew; fifteen times in Mark; thirty-three times in Luke; twice in John (3:3, 5); seven times in Acts, and occasionally in the Epistles. In this expression the word "Kingdom" has no longer a fixed meaning. In some of the passages it means the rule of God; in others, the whole sphere in which that rule is exercised; and in others again it has an ethical or spiritual meaning, as representing the state of blessedness pertaining to the Divine rule. John 3:3, 5 affords a notable instance of this third category. Scripture would never say "Except a man be born again he cannot see the Kingdom of Heaven." Still more incongruous would it be to say "he cannot see the Church." Many things may be predicted of both the Kingdom of Heaven and of the Kingdom of God; just as of England and of the British Empire. But though the terms may often be used interchangeably, they are not synonymous.

This will appear very plainly if we examine the passage in Matthew where the term "the Kingdom of God" occurs. They are chaps, 6:33; 12:28; 19:24; 21:31 and 43. The intelligent student of Scripture will see that in no one of these passages could "the Kingdom of Heaven" be used.

Chap. 16:19 claims special notice. It has been said that if these words had not been written the apostasy of Rome could never have arisen. If the distinction I am pleading for were recognized, the pretensions of Rome would collapse. It was in relation to the Earthly Messianic Kingdom that the Lord conferred upon Peter this "power of the keys." To talk of "the Keys of the Kingdom of God" is absurd. More silly still does it seem to the intelligent Christian to talk of the Keys of the Church which is the body of Christ. But Rome, though claiming to be the inspired keeper of the truth, is ignorant of these distinctions, albeit they are so obvious and so elementary.

In no case can the term "Church of God" be used interchangeably with "Kingdom of Heaven." For the one means a company of people, and the other a system of Government. The English word "Church" has meanings which the Greek word Ecclesia does not possess. In the LXX. *Ecclesia* is the usual rendering for the Hebrew *Kahal* (as 'Adah is usually rendered *sunagoge*). And whether in the LXX., in the New Testament, or in classical Greek it means only and always a company of privileged or representative people. Acts 19:32, 39, 41 may appear an exception, but we who are used to hearing an election mob addressed as "gentlemen" need not wonder if a Greek official flattered an Ephesian mob by the use of the word *Ecclesia*. And the English rendering of 1 Tim. 3:15 may also seem an exception. But there, as in verses 4, 5, and 12 of the same chapter, the word house is used by a common figure of speech for household. Paul so uses the word again in 1 Cor. 1:16; and it is so used in several passages in Acts. The language of 1 Pet. 2:5 cannot be strained to support the figment that a building would ever be an *Ecclesia*.

It is noteworthy that the word occurs nowhere in the Gospels save in Matt. 16:18, and 18:17. And I deprecate any exposition of these passages which makes them refer exclusively, or even primarily, to the present dispensation. Such an exegesis is, I think, refuted by the fact that it is in the teaching of the First Gospel that these words are recorded. But may I here hazard the opinion that a right understanding of our Lord's words in Matt. 16:16-19 would suffice to undermine the whole fabric of the apostate religion of Christendom?

In the Epistles to the Ephesians and Colossians the word *ecclesia* acquires a new dignity. In every other occurrence of it in the New Testament, and always in the LXX, it represents a company of people on earth. But in Ephesians and Colossians it includes saints on earth and saints in heaven. Having regard to 1 Cor. 12:12, some would maintain that the body means only the saints on earth. But the closing words of Eph. 1 ("His body, the fullness of Him that filleth all in all") precludes any such limitation. And the language of Ephesians and Colossians vetoes the suggestion that the term "body" is merely an illustration of the union between Christ and the Church. It is a figure, of course; but we must distinguish between a figure which is the expression of a fact and a figure which is merely an illustration of a fact. The union between Christ and those who are members of His body must be more real, not less real, than the union between a man and the members of his natural body.

Appendix

www.ingramcontent.com/pod-product-compliance
Ingram Content Group UK Ltd.
Pitfield, Milton Keynes, MK11 3LW, UK
UKHW022227230426
12048UKWH00016BA/1100